Davis

Laura Moser

HAUS PUBLISHING · LONDON

First published in Great Britain in 2004 by
Haus Publishing Limited
26 Cadogan Court
Draycott Avenue
London SW3 3BX

A CIP catalogue record for this book is available from the British Library

ISBN 1-904341-48-9

Printed and bound by Graphicom in Vicenza, Italy

Front cover: Courtesy of the Lebrecht Picture Collection / Interfoto
Back cover: Courtesy of the Lebrecht Picture Collection / Interfoto

Contents

An Actress from New England · 1908–1930

AN ABSOLUTE DESPOT

Mother Goddam, Battle-Axe Bette, Hurricane Bette, the Fourth Warner Brother, the First Lady of the Screen, the Yankee Dame, the Duse of the Depression, the Little Brown Wren, Popeye the Magnificent, the Fiery Filly, Wide-Eyed Bernhardt, Catherine the Great of Burbank, the Actress You Love to Hate, the World's Best Bette Davis Imitator: over a career that spanned half a century, Bette Davis answered to various names, both off the screen and on, but in the beginning she was just Ruth Elizabeth Davis. The year of her birth, 1908, coincides with two defining events of the American Century: the Ford Motor Company manufactured its first Model-T, and the pioneers of the film industry, headed by Thomas Edison, combined to form the Motion Picture Patents Company. The Model-T represented the invention of the modern assembly line; the Edison Trust the invention of the modern motion picture.

Edison unveiled the Kinetoscope – a single-viewer device in which short reels of film up to one minute in duration were viewed through a peep-hole – at the Chicago World Fair in 1893. As much an entrepreneur as an inventor, Edison had initially ranked the Kinetoscope low on his list of achievements, a passing amusement-arcade novelty for the illiterate masses. But when the Lumière brothers first projected a film on to a screen in 1895, he swiftly saw the market potential of his invention. In the early years of the century, as nickelodeons – an early precursor to the modern cinema, which charged 5 cents for admission – began to pop up in all the major cities of America, Edison began issuing patent lawsuits against them, to little avail. He eventually compromised with the nine leading film producers by establishing the Motion Picture Patents Company (or the 'Trust'), an umbrella organisation that forbade its members from selling or leasing equipment to any distributors who purchased pictures from other companies; Kodak in turn agreed to sell film stock only to members of the Edison Trust. As a result, a tiny group controlled every aspect of moviemaking, from production to distribution and exhibition. The Supreme Court would soon dissolve the exclusionary Trust, but similar 'vertically integrated' monopolies in the movie industry would crop up in its wake, and indeed the Hollywood studio system would later evolve along almost identical lines.

Bette Davis, more than any other actress of her generation, came of age with her industry. She was apprenticed in the film business in the 1930s, while the studios were still experimenting with talking pictures; her greatest screen successes coincided with the pinnacle of Hollywood's Golden Age; and as the studio system unravelled, so did Davis's stardom.

In the first years of Davis's life, while Hollywood was taking shape on the other edge of the continent as the international centre of movie production, the inhabitants of her hometown of Lowell, Massachusetts, had little knowledge of its innovations and little leisure to explore them. Davis's parents cut prominent figures against Lowell's grim industrial landscape, as both belonged to New England families with Yankee pedigrees dating back to the 17th century: Davis's father, Harlow Morrell Davis, descended from Welsh Puritans; her mother, Ruth Favor, from Huguenot pioneers. The couple first met when Harlow was seven and Ruthie six, at an open-air gospel service held by the Free Baptists, one of the many populist religious movements sweeping America after the Civil War. Fifteen years later, soon after finishing university, Harlow Davis proposed to his old family friend.

Once a strong-willed tomboy who dreamt of becoming an

The five month old Ruth Elizabeth Davis in 1909. Bette was born with little more than a good Yankee pedigree, much of her childhood was lived in poverty.

actress, by age 20 Ruthie had already recognised the impractical-ity of her aspirations. While her brothers attended Ivy League universities, Ruthie's education centred on attracting a man of Harlow's precise description – clever, ambitious, patrician. She accepted his offer with little equivocation. When, only a few weeks after their wedding on 1 July 1907, Ruthie announced that she was pregnant, Harlow – preoccupied as he was with entering Harvard Law School that autumn – warned his new wife that he could not yet provide for a family of two, much less three. Ruthie, however, still took her religious upbringing seriously, and rejected his suggestion that she abort with horror.

Born on 5 April 1908, nine months almost to the day after her parents' wedding, Ruth Elizabeth Davis started life in combat, or so she liked to think. *I have been at war from the beginning*, she writes in the first paragraph of her 1961 autobiography, *The*

Lonely Life. I rode into the field with sword gleaming and banner flying.[1]

Reality, alas, fell far short of these Arthurian fantasies. While Harlow struggled through law school and Ruthie scrimped to stretch every dollar, the young couple bickered often, then incessantly: Bette Davis later claimed not to *recall one moment of affection* between her parents.[2] The birth, in late 1909, of Barbara Harriet or 'Bobby' Davis, did little to repair the foundering marriage, and in 1911 – the same year that Harlow took a well-paying job at the United Shoe Machinery Corporation of Boston (where he worked as a patent attorney until his death 25 years later) – Ruthie checked into a sanatorium. She later blamed her condition on her husband's cruelty and neglect, but Harlow did not leave until 1918, several weeks before his older daughter's tenth birthday. 'If a man gets a cup of coffee thrown in his face every morning, he can't keep his self-respect,'[3] remains the only explanation he offered for leaving when he did.

Harlow Davis's *cavalier disappearance* profoundly altered the psychology of his famous daughter.[4] But though its significance cannot be overstated in understanding her personality – particularly her lifelong difficulties with men – in 1918 Davis dismissed her father with typical bravado, applauding: *Now we can go on a picnic and have a baby!*[5] The real baby of the family took the break-up much harder. In the tumultuous year leading up to the divorce, Bobby Davis grew so silent and withdrawn that Ruthie had to remove her from school, whereupon the eight-year-old suffered the first in a lifetime of nervous breakdowns. Ruthie, for her part, was more humiliated than heartbroken, for among the Boston Brahmins with whom she emphatically classed herself, respectable women did not get divorces. To console herself, she set about demonising her ex-husband as a curmudgeon and a crank. Bette Davis would later take cues from her mother, lamenting to countless interviewers that *I felt I never had a father.*[6]

In the year after Harlow's departure, as Ruthie slowly bounced back to life, Bobby's never-ending gloom began to grate and the lonely single mother directed more and more of her energy to her resilient, charismatic older daughter. Though many judged Bobby the prettier of the Davis girls, in the Davis family photographs of this era Ruthie time and again relegated her younger daughter to the back corner of the frame, or omitted her altogether. Betty was Ruthie's inspiration and sole salvation.

People believed spare the rod and spoil the child, Davis once said when asked about her upbringing, *but my mother always felt I could conquer any goal, and said so.*[7] But if Ruthie's passion instilled in young Betty Davis the imperious self-regard that would later fuel her climb to fame, it also strengthened some less desirable characteristics. *I became an absolute despot at the age of two*, Davis said.[8] In 1909, while still a toddler, Betty was so offended by the birth of her younger sister that she chopped off the newborn's hair, an act of infantile aggression that would set the tone for the siblings' relationship throughout their lives.

Betty was headstrong from the beginning, tackling even hobbies with the utmost seriousness. *I became the most dedicated Girl Scout that ever lived. I would have tripped an old lady in order to pick her up.*[9] In matters of dress, she was a perfectionist, refusing to wear clothes twice and crying whenever dirt spotted her shoes. *To this day, I would walk over burning coals to straighten a picture, to adjust a blind*, she would later write in her autobiography.[10] Proud of this fastidiousness, the actress often told interviewers about a rare outing her family had once made to the circus. Even Harlow was enjoying himself until Betty, four at the time, noticed a crooked seam in the carpet of the animal runway. The asymmetry and sloppiness so disconcerted the child that she pitched a violent fit and forced her parents to return home early.

Harlow had never hesitated to scold Betty for being an *ungrateful brat*, but after he left, no one else dared challenge her extravagant responses to life's passing annoyances.[11] Ruthie, on the contrary, indulged her older daughter's every outburst and submitted to even her most absurd caprice, so that Betty grew up accustomed to absolute power and well versed in its abuses. Harlow had not been gone two years before Betty's lack of respect for authority first landed her in serious trouble. It was December 1919, and the 11-year-old had dressed up as Father Christmas for her school's holiday party. Ignoring parents' and teachers' admonitions to avoid the massive wax candles lighting the Christmas tree, Betty lunged for a box with her name on it, and in her haste brushed against one of the candles. The sleeve of her costume caught fire, and she collapsed writhing on to the floor. Teachers wrapped her in a blanket to extinguish the flames while cries of 'She's blind! Dear God, she's blind!' swirled around her.

I was in complete control of the moment, she recalled decades later. *I had never known such power.*[12] Savouring the *morbid pleasure* of her audience's terror, she lingered there long after the blanket had been lifted, her eyes squeezed shut, no less transformed than if she had been blinded.[13] That night, beneath shut lids, Bette Davis came face-to-face with what she would call *the one, great, durable romance* of her life: centre stage.[14]

This incident (a fitting debut for one of the most famous smokers of the 20th century) showcases qualities that would bring Bette Davis adoration and notoriety in the ensuing decades: her demand for attention, even at the price of cruelty, and her desire for *complete control*. Its aftermath suggests how these traits became so prominent.

At Grand Central Station the morning after the accident, Ruthie Davis had trouble recognising her older daughter through the bubble-wrap of burnt skin. Doctors advised the terrified mother that, without a full-time nurse to swab the blisters and change the bandages every two hours, the girl would be scarred for life. Ruthie was poor, but if she couldn't afford a full-time nurse, she could play one. She set her alarm clock and spent the next two weeks tending the wounds. Throughout the delirious vigil, Ruthie funnelled her own thwarted ambitions into her patient, regaling her daughter with fantastic promises of glamour and stardom. In the end, Ruthie's ministrations paid off, and Betty emerged from her mummification with what would become her greatest asset on camera: a transparent, glowing complexion. The most significant result of her convalescence, however, was psychological: when Betty Davis shook off her bandages, it was with a new faith in the power she exercised over her mother – and of the 'special fate' that awaited them both.[15]

Bette and her sister 'Bobby' Davis ca. 1917

This conviction would prove indispensable in the poverty-ridden years that followed. Over the course of that decade, the 'Three Musketeers' – as Ruthie called their reconfigured, all-female family – embarked on a picaresque course across the Eastern Seaboard, moving an estimated 80 times between 1918 and 1930. To supplement Harlow's monthly alimony cheque of $200, which was a pittance even in 1918, Ruthie worked as a governess, a dormitory cleaner, a boarding-school house mother – any job, in short, that allowed her to place her daughters in the best schools for the lowest fees. Her rare moments of leisure she devoted to elevating her old hobby, portrait photography, into a higher-paying, more prestigious trade.

After a brief separation that the girls spent in a modest boarding school – the site of Betty's run-in with the candles – in 1921 Ruthie moved her daughters to a small room on 144th Street and Broadway, the heart of Harlem at the dawn of its renaissance, so that she could enrol in a photography course in Manhattan.

Among the girls' exotic new acquaintances was an erudite neighbour who admired Balzac's *Cousine Bette*. It was she who suggested that Betty, who was already keen to stand out from the crowd, change the spelling of her name. Betty did so eagerly, but if she had expected this re-christening to trigger any rebirth, she was sorely disappointed. As the Musketeers continued wandering from boarding house to bed-sit, Ruthie never lost sight of her central objective – to provide her daughters with all the privileges due to the children of a successful patent attorney – but still the nomadic lifestyle took a heavy toll on the adolescent children. After Harlem, Ruthie accepted a job as a photo developer in suburban New Jersey. It was here that Bette Davis, at the age of 15, hit bottom. To withstand the indignity of sharing a dingy boarding house attic with her mother and sister and breaking bread with strangers, the teenager existed *in a static mist . . . punctuated by occasional rages*.[16]

These rages soon sapped Ruthie's strength. Falling ill with osteomyelitis of the jaw, a bone inflammation caused by bacterial infection, the tired mother retreated to the safety of Massachusetts, where budget restrictions landed the girls in a large school in the Boston suburb of Newton. Though Bette Davis was an undisputed hit at Newton High School, popular with both male and female classmates, the socially ambitious Ruthie still thought her daughters too refined for a state-subsidised education, and as soon as she was earning money as a photographer again transferred them to the only private institution in her price range, a conservative parochial boarding school. Bette and Bobby were both so miserable there that Ruthie had to move them again after a single semester, this time to the more exclusive (and expensive) Cushing Academy.

Bette Davis flourished at Cushing even more than at Newton – in the upper-crust setting she had found her *milieu* at last. Honour student and social sensation, elected president of her sorority and voted prettiest girl in the class, she even fell in love for the first time. Harmon Oscar 'Ham' Nelson, a soft-spoken jazz musician, was a passive creature, content to stand back and watch as his girlfriend racked up awards and admirers. Davis's good fortune persisted through the summer of 1925, which the trio spent in the small artistic community of Peterborough, New Hampshire. As a dance pupil at the town's second-tier school – the best that Ruthie could afford – Davis attracted the attention of Roshanara, an exotic, India-reared Englishwoman who taught at the famous Mariarden colony. Impressed by the girl's lithe, expressive movements, Roshanara proposed to exchange Bette's tuition for Bobby's piano-playing services. All three Musketeers rejoiced: Ruthie for the advancement of her vicarious dream, Bobby for her five-dollar-a-week contribution to the family coffers, Bette for this outside acknowledgement of her genius. After rehearsing all summer for eight hours a day, the 17-year-old gave her first performance before a paying public in late July 1925; among the dazzled audience was the theatre director Frank Conroy, who told Ruthie that it would be a 'crime' to keep Davis off the stage.[17]

As a teenager attending Newton High, Davis, in an effort to contribute to the family finances, posed for a statue of Spring, completely nude. In 1982, a rip-roaring 'Bette Davis Statue Hunt' was initiated in Massachusetts. The statue was finally discovered in the basement of the Museum of Fine Arts in Boston.

Davis dedicated the following year, her last at Cushing, to her new gift. She starred in several school plays and even the climactic senior pageant, while her mother worked overtime to meet tuition costs. When despite her best efforts Ruthie failed to raise enough money, the headmaster suggested that Davis wait tables in the student dining room. It was a crushing comedown for the Prettiest Girl of the Class of 1926, and it took many years for Davis to recast this humiliation as one of the *great lessons* of her difficult adolescence.[18] Ruthie had to cover the remaining deficit by volunteering as senior class photographer. She spent the next weeks locked inside her darkroom, forsaking food and sleep to develop, print and retouch every portrait. Ruthie's slavish commitment saw its reward when, at the 1926 Cushing graduation ceremony, Bette received her diploma with the rest of her class. From her position on the stage, Bette could see Ruthie in the audience looking more faded than a haggard washerwoman; then and there the 18-year-old vowed that one day her mother would never have to work again.

In later life the scale of these sacrifices would more and more haunt Davis, who once remarked that Ruthie *let us wreck her personal life . . . She never thought of herself, only of us.*[19] In time Davis even came to sympathise with her father's *indignation* with Ruthie, his *contempt* for her overbearing personality.[20] *Ruthie had raised Bobby and me in such a strait-laced way,* Davis said in 1980, *that we had to get her okay to go to the bathroom.*[21] As Davis enjoyed her first theatrical successes, her mother's non-stop support soon became a hindrance, then an all-out embarrassment. 'She was always around', one of Davis's first directors said, calling Ruthie 'the archetype of the classic stage mother – only worse'.[22]

Perhaps even more inconvenienced by Ruthie's love affair with her older daughter was Bobby Davis, who suffered more egregious neglect every year. The summer after Davis finished high school, in 1926, Ruthie and Bette dumped Bobby with an obliging neighbour so that the two of them could hole up in a tiny cottage and plot Bette Davis's rise to fame. That fall, Bobby re-entered the public high school in Newton – the same institution that, only two years earlier, Ruthie had judged unsuitable for her more gifted daughter. After graduating from Newton High School, almost wholly unsupervised, Bobby won a scholarship to Dennison University in Ohio, the first of many attempts to build a life beyond her mother's and older sister's monomania. None would succeed.

ALL BIG EYES AND TALENT

Following high school, Davis sank into a period of inactivity while Ruthie worked to save money in the vague hope of one day funding her daughter's theatrical training. From the autumn of 1926 through the next spring, as her better-heeled friends trickled off one by one to university, Davis became deeply depressed. Her spirits revived only once that whole year, when Ruthie took her to see Henrik Ibsen's *The Wild Duck*. The intensity of her identification with the juvenile lead, Hedvig – a trusting girl destroyed by her father's desertion – rekindled Davis's confidence: *I knew now that more than anything – despite anything – I was going to become an actress.*[23]

Like the fictional Hedvig, Bette Davis had been damaged by her father's abandonment. Though he was wealthy and successful by 1926, Harlow Morrell Davis, who had long since remarried, still denied his first family a penny more than the $200 a month ordered by the 1918 divorce settlement. Generous only with opinions, Harlow spent his rare visits denouncing Davis's ambitions, ordering that she choose a 'sensible' job – something secretarial, say – instead. Davis credited her obstinate defiance of this advice with Harlow's abrupt decision, a few months after her high-school graduation, to revise his will. In leaving his entire estate to his second wife, he was careful to avoid all ambiguity: 'This I do to the absolute exclusion of my children, Ruth Elizabeth Davis and Barbara Harriet Davis.'[24]

To offset such a gloomy year, in the summer of 1927 Ruthie

carted her daughters to Cape Cod, where she worked as a house-keeper in exchange for a rent-free cabin. For Bette, the only female in the bustling seaside town to pass the lifeguard certification tests, those enchanted months were the 'last carefree summer', in Ruthie's words, of her life.[25] Having lost touch with her Cushing boyfriend Ham, Davis dated several dashing Ivy Leaguers before falling in love with Fritz Hall, a student at Yale University. As this blissful summer drew to a close – some 15 months after Davis's graduation from Cushing – Ruthie decided that her daughter's time had come at last.

After leaving Bobby with another relative in Newton, Ruthie led Bette into the bright lights of the Big Apple, determined that, once and for all, the two of them would *storm Broadway*.[26] Ruthie had fixed on the Eva La Gallienne Civic Repertory Company both for its unimpeachable reputation and, more importantly, for its scholarship programme, which enabled students to earn their own tuition by performing in company productions. But after La Gallienne asked 19-year-old Davis to read the part of an elderly Dutch woman, the redoubtable teacher abruptly dismissed the applicant as a 'frivolous little girl', a slight that Davis never forgot.[27] *La Gallienne*, Davis recalled, *made me feel stupid and I wasn't prepared for that.*[28] Ruthie had no choice but to return to Boston in defeat.

This brusque rejection demolished what little happiness Davis had found that summer in Cape Cod, and once back in Boston, she once again despaired about her suburban doom. *I was in a backwash, going nowhere, and I saw no hope of any change.*[29] Meanwhile, Ruthie – whose acquaintance with discouragement spanned much longer – secured a job as a photo retoucher in a Connecticut town much closer to New York. Davis passed her days hunched in the diner opposite Ruthie's photo shop, watching in horror as her mother executed repetitive, degrading tasks. One morning in late October 1927, Davis was asleep in her bed

– where she spent a great deal of her time – when Ruthie shook her awake and hustled her on to the train to New York. Too torpid for second-guessing, Davis trailed her mother from Grand Central, straight through the front doors of the Anderson School of the Theatre. There Davis just sat, slack-jawed and silent, listening to Ruthie persuade Anderson's directors to admit her with no guarantee of payment. Davis began classes that same afternoon.

Martha Graham Davis's teacher and lifelong muse

In the late 1920s, the Anderson School was a revolutionary training ground that was to prime many of Davis's contemporaries – Paul Muni, Katharine Hepburn, and Lucille Ball – for stardom. Rather than glamorise the actor's life, Anderson teachers deployed scare tactics to weed out the less dedicated pupils. Testimonies of hardship only redoubled Bette's ambition: she had struggled to get this far, why give up now?

It was during her first semester at Anderson that Davis really began to develop her skills as an actress. Under the tutelage of Martha Graham, she experimented with her gesture-heavy, body-emphatic style of acting. Davis revered the legendary dancer, whose controversial theories about the connection between physicality and self-expression – the 'syntax' of the body – would become central to Davis's technique. *I use everything at my command when I act*, Davis said, and indeed, in her best performances, she relied principally on the movements of her arms and head, thrashing and whipping and shivering.[30] She also shed her Boston accent at Anderson, perfecting the clipped tone that so many would learn to imitate.

The prim Bostonian enjoyed her first taste of adult independence that first year in New York. Ruthie visited frequently, sleeping on two chairs pushed together so as not to disturb the blooming thespian's beauty rest, but the rest of the time Davis explored Jazz Age Manhattan unsupervised. The Theatre District – back then, host to groundbreaking premieres of plays by George Bernard Shaw, Eugene O'Neill and Noel Coward, with Shakespeare on regular rotation – supplied endless stimulation.

Dramatic school is important only for the basic education it imparts. The alphabet must be learned. How to move. How to sit and stand . . . But knowing all the letters from A to Zed does not make one a writer . . . There are things that cannot be taught. Or rather, there are things that cannot be learned. Davis concludes her retrospective assessment of theatre school with a telling dismissal: *For the talentless, it is true that a chart gives them direction.*

Bette Davis, *The Lonely Life*[31]

Soon at the top of her class, Davis won a $500 scholarship to cover the next semester's tuition. That same week, she also landed her first part in a professional production, *The Earth Between.* Forced to choose between training and fame, she chucked the scholarship and dropped out of school, but no sooner had she burned her bridges with Anderson than the director of *The Earth Between* announced the indefinite postponement of the production, leaving Davis with no diploma, no scholarship, no job, and no money.

Through contacts, the desperate actress found a short-term job as a last-minute replacement in George Cukor's summer stock ensemble in upstate New York. Little did Davis realise at the time, but the man who led this highly respected Rochester repertory company would become one of the master directors of Hollywood's Golden Age. Her abjection postponed, Davis regretted only that her mother was unable to supervise her first professional engagement. Hawk-eyed Ruthie, stuck at the New Jersey boarding school where she was working to support Davis, hastened to dispatch a compendium of instructions and warnings to her immaculate daughter: advice on which garments to pack and when to unpack them; which toiletries to purchase and when to use them; how to board a train and how to undress inside it; how to cross one's legs and when not to raise one's eyes. Davis did her best to obey her mother's diktats, even an instruction that she memorise the lead actress's lines. Sure enough, on the last night of the season, the lead actress fell and twisted her ankle only a few hours before curtain-up. To Cukor's astonishment, his shy stand-in offered her services immediately. With no preparation, Davis delivered such a brilliant performance that Cukor invited her to join the company as the ingénue (the youngest female member of a repertory group, assigned to play the younger sisters and daughters and naïve first-time lovers) that autumn.

Penniless until the new season commenced, Davis returned to Manhattan in early August of 1928 to badger casting agencies for work, but for all her tenacity she met with no luck. After several weeks, and with considerable relief, Davis heard of another ingénue position at the Cape Playhouse in Cape Cod, Massachusetts. It seemed an auspicious coincidence, for she remembered her previous summer in Cape Cod as the happiest of her life.

Davis arrived in high spirits, only to find that the company needed not an ingénue but an usherette. Would Miss Davis oblige? Every night, as she showed the spectators to their seats, she *dreamed of sprained ankles*.[32]

After almost an entire summer of this drudgery, Davis seized an opening when Laura Hope Crews, a famous stage actress who was directing a play, judged the usual ingénue inappropriate for a part. Crews agreed to endure Davis's audition only if the unspectacular usherette could learn an obscure English ballad overnight. Because the prima donna director failed to supply the sheet music, Ruthie was forced to comb every music store in eastern Massachusetts for the long out-of-print song. By dusk, the weary mother was banging on the doors of private homes with pianos visible from the street. It was only when she burst into a small church a few miles from the Playhouse that Ruthie found not only the sheet music, but also an avuncular organist willing to rehearse until 3 in the morning. Even after Davis got the part, Crews continued to discipline her young recruit severely, slapping her palms and cringing at the pronunciation. But Davis had her revenge in the end, winning ecstatic praise from the critics. By the end of the summer of 1928, Bette Davis had proved her invincibility yet again.

Back with Cukor's repertory company in Rochester that September, Davis concentrated on mastering a new role every week. She became so absorbed in her work, that she neglected to cultivate her colleagues' friendship and never noticed the factions forming against her. Only the ill-concealed distaste of fellow ensemble member Miriam Hopkins (1902–1972) upset Davis's concentration. Davis would encounter Hopkins – a classically beautiful and relentlessly belligerent Southern Belle – time and again in her later career. Davis was understandably astonished, when, after only a half-dozen performances – all of them well received – Cukor sacked her, citing her deficient team spirit. *Let's be frank about this,* the actress hissed in self-defence, *team spirit is for those who don't aspire to much.*[33] At the time, she attributed the injustice to her refusal to 'mix' with the men in Cukor's company. Raised a *chaste and modest New England maiden*, Davis recoiled from the standard 'casting couch' auditions.[34] *That's why I'm so thankful I never had to rely on looks*, she said of her unfashionable morality. *I survived on talent and temperament. If I'd had to make it on the casting couch, I'd have screamed 'Rape!' and that would have ended my career!*[35]

No, the path to greatness permitted no mixing. Davis had already proven her immunity to the snares and seductions that had brought down many actresses before her. She had continued to date Fritz Hall, the Yale student she met while staying on Cape Cod in the summer of 1927, through into 1928. Then, in spring of 1928, at the height of her intoxication with the Anderson School, Hall proposed. Davis wore the engagement ring for three days before her blue-blooded fiancé announced that he required not a professional entertainer but a 'wife and hostess'.[36] Ruthie immediately swooped on to the scene to warn against the engagement, enumerating the dangers of sacrificing ambition – nay, greatness – for convention. Davis split with Hall the same afternoon.

'Ruthie had done her work well,' Davis's roommate recalled. 'Bette had avoided her first temptation to bask in romantic domesticity. Now she was well and truly set upon her career.'[38] Ruthie had taught her daughter that the 'real' actress marries only her art, or, as Davis put it toward the end of her life, *I've always been an actress first and a woman second*.[39]

In late 1928, back in Manhattan after the Rochester setback, Davis was fighting off another wave of depression when

The work of director George Cukor (1899–1983) in Hollywood includes such hits as *The Philadelphia Story* (1941), *Gaslight* (1944), *A Star is Born* (1956) and *My Fair Lady* (which won him the Best Director Oscar in 1965). Throughout his long career, the openly gay director was celebrated for his 'feminine touch', drawing exceptional performances from his female leads, from Greta Garbo and Judy Garland to Ingrid Bergman and Marilyn Monroe. But after their brief encounter in Rochester he never worked with Bette Davis again. 'Her talent was apparent,' Cukor said, 'but she did buck at direction.'[37]

Bette Davis the modest New England
maiden ca. 1926

director James Light contacted her about *The Earth Between*, the play that Davis had quit school to join the previous spring. The production was off the ground at last, and Light still wanted Davis for the juvenile lead.

She and Ruthie moved into a small apartment in Greenwich Village, then the capital of American Bohemia, the pilgrimage point of artists and runaways and revolutionaries. At the centre of this neighbourhood stood the Provincetown Playhouse, known as the 'Theatre of Opportunity' for its instrumental role in jump-starting the careers of several famous actors, including Paul Robeson and Al Jolson. Host to experimental plays by many important modernists – among them, Eugene O'Neill, e e cummings, Theodore Dreiser, Edmund Wilson and Edna St Vincent Millay – the Provincetown Playhouse welcomed controversial fare like *The Earth Between*, the story of a young girl ensnared in an incestuous relationship with her father.

Bette Davis would later become famous playing roles shunned by 'respectable actresses', but at the age of 20, she was so sheltered that she only understood the play's racy subject matter after reading the opening-night reviews. Any anxiety she might have felt about her naïveté was quickly drowned in the critics' loud applause. Davis called the night of her New York City debut *an ecstasy that has never quite been equalled.*[40] She earned her first mention in the *New York Times* – a landmark in the career of any American artist – as an 'enchanting creature who plays in a soft, unassertive style'.[41] (Both adjectives are amusing in light of her mature excesses.) Not only did her new boyfriend, Charlie Ainsley – whom she had met soon after moving to New York – profess his love to her for the first time on the first night, but Harlow Davis, in an unprecedented gesture of approval, even sent flowers to her dressing room. Most exhilarating of all, Broadway's immortal Blanche Yurka, after seeing the production, summoned its young star to her studio and offered Davis the role of Hedvig in a touring production of *The Wild Duck* – remarkably the same role that had given Bette's obscure adolescent ambitions their first distinct shape.

Several days before *The Earth Between* closed, Davis came down with a severe case of the measles and fell feverish into bed. Terrified some trifling virus might spoil her daughter's biggest break yet, Ruthie Davis hovered over Bette's sickbed, drilling lines and rehearsing scenes while the illness ran its course. By some miracle of will, Davis recovered the morning of her scheduled opening in *The Wild Duck*. Davis rushed straight to the theatre, where she went through a single perfunctory dress rehearsal, and then – an hour into her first sortie in a fortnight – found herself before a Broadway audience for the first time. *To have been in bed for two weeks and then find myself on a stage on Broadway was too much for me to take in*, she said.[42] The leap from Greenwich Village to Broadway takes most actors decades; Davis made it in a single afternoon. The play was a smash, and critics' enthusiasm for the young lead unbounded.

Davis's boyfriend, Charlie Ainsley, had recently proposed to Davis, but then abruptly broke off their engagement seconds before *The Wild Duck* opened in Boston – her homecoming show, the proof of how far she had come. Davis certainly resented Ainsley's timing but she rose above her rage onstage. Her former higher-class friends from Newton High School were all on hand to applaud the finest performance yet from the poor nomad from a broken home.

After *The Wild Duck* tour ended, Davis spent a blissful summer at the Cape Playhouse; no longer an usherette but a prized member of the company, she was greeted with her own dressing room and a contract for the next year. But in the autumn of 1929 Davis washed up on the shores of Manhattan again, her brief run of good luck abruptly terminated. She was subsisting on meal invitations from unsavoury suitors and random acquaintances when she landed a leading role in *Broken Dishes,* a new domestic comedy on Broadway. Opening in the wake of the Stock Market Crash of 1929, before the economic catastrophes of Black October had affected the leisure class's spending habits, *Broken Dishes* was such a hit that the producers soon raised Davis's salary to an unheard-of $150 a week.

Davis was still enjoying her success in *Broken Dishes* when a scout from Samuel Goldwyn approached her for a screen test. Despite her contentment on Broadway, Davis looked forward to the trial, for she knew that, in 1929, the screen test was the stage actor's litmus of success. Experiments with sound technology had advanced throughout the decade, but it was only with the perfection of the Vitaphone system, which involved recording sound on discs, that studios could make pictures with synchronised action and dialogue. In the wake of Warner Brothers' historic release of Al Jolson's *The Jazz Singer* – the first movie to include full-length songs and snippets of dialogue – in November of 1927, the most talented of Davis's colleagues were undergoing similar auditions.

'Wait a minute, wait a minute, you ain't heard nothing yet!' Before Jolson had spoken his first sentence onscreen, most Hollywood higher-ups had dismissed talking pictures, or 'talkies', as a passing fad, much as Thomas Edison had once slighted his Kinetoscope. Chief among these nay-sayers was Warners' executive Harry Warner, who had repeatedly discouraged the project with the famous question, 'Who the hell wants to hear actors talk?'[43] When the answer turned out to be everyone, the whole industry scrambled to invest in talkies. The studios needed not just the necessary technology, but also the talent. The careers of many silent screen stars collapsed overnight – such was the fate of the fictional Lina Lamont, the photogenic goddess with the voice of a crow, in the 1952 film *Singin' in the Rain* – and studio scouts invaded Broadway in search of actors who could enunciate as well as gesticulate, sing as well as sashay. These raids yielded some of the most celebrated names of Hollywood's Golden Age: James Cagney, Clark Gable, Claudette Colbert, Humphrey Bogart, Spencer Tracy, Leslie Howard, Edward G Robinson, and, of course, Bette Davis.

Like most of her relationships, Davis's love affair with the camera started rocky. She arrived at the Goldwyn studio in Queens in early 1930 with a chipped tooth and a dowdy dress. Bewildered that no

Bette Davis made one of the most successful transformations from the Broadway stage to the sound stages of the new Hollywood 'talkies'

one attempted to dress her or powder her nose, much less direct her, Davis saw no alternative but to gape dumbly into the dark lens. Typically, Davis reacted to Goldwyn's subsequent rejection less with surprise than contempt. Too dignified for celluloid distortion, she vowed to grow old on Broadway. She soon joined another Broadway production, *Solid South*, and stuck to her word for almost a year before submitting to another screen test in late 1930, this time for Universal. Davis relented not because her hatred of Hollywood had diminished in the interim, but because Universal had dangled before her the starring role in the screen version of a hit play, *Strictly Dishonourable.* Seldom singled out in reviews of *Solid South,* Davis wanted a new challenge – or, what is more likely, a new opportunity to step into the spotlight. Since *Strictly Dishonourable* was originally a stage play, Davis regarded the property as an ideal compromise between theatre and film.

Teeth straightened and hair styled, Davis was better prepared for her second screen test, and Universal offered her a six-month contract with a staggering salary of $300 a week. Davis quashed her misgivings about Hollywood and signed up. A few days later, a Universal publicity man pressed her to feminise her unglamorous name for the screen. He suggested 'Bettina Dawes', causing the frail-looking nymphet to flame: *Bettina Dawes*! *I refuse to be called 'Between the Drawers' all my life!*[44]

The subject never came up again, but the disagreement resurrected all of Davis's old doubts. Were her sophisticated Broadway friends right to scorn the film industry? Had she just sold out on her promise as a 'real' actress? Would Hollywood succeed in reshaping her as it had so many others?

The Dream Factory · 1931–1934

Davis came to Hollywood during some of the film industry's most transformative years. In late 1930, when she arrived at Universal City, a 230-acre film factory built on mustard fields only 15 years earlier, she ranked her new employer among the most prestigious of Hollywood studios. But though Universal had recently won the Best Picture Oscar for *All Quiet on the Western Front*, 43 years would pass before the studio won another major Academy Award. The Great Depression, triggered by the Wall Street Crash of October 1929, had changed everything.

Buoyed by the technological developments and boom in ticket sales of the 1920s, the film industry had seemed immune to the nationwide economic collapse. 1929 was Hollywood's most successful year yet: a population of 123 million (in the 1930 census) was buying around 100 million cinema tickets every week. The growing ranks of the unemployed, if unable to afford food, still managed the 15-cents price of admission every week: the less money Americans had, the more they sought escape in the empire of shadows, flocking to gangster films, musicals, screwball comedies and racy bedroom dramas. 'During the Depression, when the spirit of the people is lower than at any other time,' opined President Roosevelt himself, 'it is a splendid thing that for just 15 cents an American can go to a movie and look at the smiling face of a baby and forget his troubles.'[45]

Depression-era movies offered downtrodden Americans not just escapism but the promise of redemption. Hollywood's optimistic messages and tidy morals worked to restore the nation's mythical values of individualism, classlessness and progress. Through the lens of cinema, recovery seemed not just possible but imminent, inevitable. Will Hays, head of the Motion Picture Producers and Distributors of America, Hollywood's chief censorship operation, commended the industry's social utility in this respect: 'No medium has contributed more greatly than the film to the maintenance of the national morale during a period featured by revolution, riot and political turmoil in other countries.'[46]

But as the Depression dragged on and unemployment hit an all-time high in 1933, with a quarter of the country out of work, audiences began to tail off and box office sales soon dropped by almost 40 per cent. As their hefty profits turned to debts, the movie moguls shut down a third of the nation's cinemas, most of which had opened in the previous five years. In a bid to keep the ever-dwindling audiences entertained, the surviving cinemas were forced to change their programmes as often as twice a week. As studios released more films on smaller budgets, movie production became a far grimmer affair. With salaries slashed by 50 per cent, the glory days of grooming stars, polishing scripts, close-ups, retakes and professional editors came to an abrupt end.

Bette Davis was as appalled by these cut-rate, assembly-line production methods as by the sexual exploitation rampant in Hollywood. She spent her first days in Hollywood draped over a series of divans, grinning and blinking for endless 'cheesecake' publicity photos. No less disappointed with their new recruit than Davis was with the studio, Universal further insulted her by giving another actress the lead in *Strictly Dishonourable*, the film that had lured Davis across the continent. She was cast instead in *Bad Sister* as the dull foil to the hell-raising title character's antics. Seeing herself onscreen for the first time at the *Bad Sister* preview, Davis burst into tears and fled the cinema. Even less impressed, her bosses soon nicknamed her 'Little Brown Wren' for her ash-blonde hair and general drabness.

Seed, Waterloo Bridge, Way Back Home, The Menace, Hell's House –

Davis turned out five more movies in her first six months at Universal, all as dismal as her debut. Fast frustrated with her mousy typecasting and 'poor cousin'[47] treatment in Universal City, Davis stayed on for the money. Her sister, Bobby, had recently been hospitalised with what is today known as manic-depressive illness. The deluge of medical bills struck Broadway off Davis's list of options. Bobby's psychiatric upkeep would continue to drain her sister's income over the next half century. As late as 1964, Davis was complaining to an interviewer about the expense of her sister's repeated hospitalisations: *Bobby has flipped her wig again, and is in the hospital in Phoenix. As usual, it will cost me a fortune.*[48]

Living in Hollywood was costly and Davis's expenses skyrocketed with her salary. Early on it was, curiously enough, Ruthie Davis who posed the most persistent threat to Davis's financial stability. Well before Davis received her first paycheque from Universal, the former housekeeper insisted on renting a massive (and massively overpriced) house, which she deemed indispensable to the public image of a rising young star. Ruthie next requested a splendid car, an extravagant all-new wardrobe and, in time, an even larger house and an even more modern car. So it went on over the decades. *Now she was going to rest on my laurels, and rest in elegance,* Davis said of Ruthie. *She not only became my daughter, she became a spoiled daughter. She was lovely, fractious, indolent, and increasingly self-absorbed. She always spent more than I could earn, and she was indifferent to my daily struggles. I don't think she believed I worked a day once I arrived.*[49] The martyr-mother never worked again, only spent, refusing to adjust her needs to her daughter's earnings, least of all during Davis's periodic unpaid suspensions. Ruthie was finally living like a top attorney's wife should, and she had no intention of surrendering a single frill.

Then, in September of 1931, only nine months after Davis arrived in Pasadena, Universal set the Little Brown Wren free by

Ruth Davis was her daughter's greatest champion and became her heaviest burden, here they arrive cocooned in mink at the premiere of *All About Eve* in November 1950

deciding not to renew her contract. The actress crumpled, for if she disliked anything more than film, it was failure. She was already preparing to return to New York when the phone rang. On the other end of the line was the venerated English actor George Arliss, Hollywood's closest approximation to royalty in 1931, calling to offer Davis a meaty role in *The Man Who Played God* at Warner Brothers. In spite of Warners' dubious reputation, the cut in her salary, and the one-picture-only deal, Davis rejoiced. For the rest of her life she called *The Man Who Played God* the 'most important part'[50] of her career: by no means her most nuanced or challenging vehicle, but the stroke of luck that secured her home in Hollywood. In the film, Davis played Grace, a young girl enamoured of Arliss's character, a once-famous concert pianist recently deafened by a tragic accident. However unlikely a match the 23-year-old actress seemed for the 63-year-old Arliss, Davis attracted the attention of Warners' executives with her subtle, never silly, portrayal of the naïve and self-sacrificing girl. Critics also took notice of Davis, 'a vision of wide-eyed blonde beauty'; several even mistook the Little Brown Wren, whose hair now blazed platinum, for glamorous.[51]

In December of 1931, almost exactly a year after migrating to the West Coast, Bette Davis signed a multi-picture contract with Warner Brothers. She was to remain at the studio for the next 18 years. They were the greatest years of her career and indeed of her life – the years that transformed Bette Davis into a legend.

THE WARNERS' STABLE

'We're not running any museum,' Jack Warner liked to say of the film studio that he and his three brothers Harry, Albert and Sam had founded in 1923.[52] Like many of the early Hollywood moguls, the Warners were first-generation Americans, Jews of Polish descent. The enterprising brothers – sons of a travelling salesman, each born in a different North American depot – first entered the film business running nickelodeon cinemas in 1910. After minor successes distributing films made by others, they progressed to producing their own short films, and released their first feature in 1915.

The only family-run firm – and by far the youngest of the major studios – Warner Brothers established its credentials in the industry by focusing on advances in sound technology. The studio made Hollywood history in 1926 with *Don Juan*, the first film to incorporate synchronised music and sound effects, and the following year gambled big on Al Jolson's *The Jazz Singer*, which increased

Warners' assets exponentially (from 5 million in 1925 to 230 million in 1930) and rocketed the studio into Hollywood's 'Big Five' alongside Paramount, Lowe's, RKO and Metro-Goldwyn Mayer. (Columbia, Universal and United Artists were grouped separately, as the 'Little Three'.)

After *The Jazz Singer*, the Warners preferred to draw meagre profits from many films rather than risk large sums on potentially disastrous blockbusters. Warners produced pictures on the tightest budgets of any major studio, and soon lagged far behind its competitors in developments like Technicolor. The studio also saved money by producing low-risk adaptations of popular fiction that had been 'pre-tested' in the marketplace. Bette Davis once summed up this formulaic treatment of plot with the wry observation: *We had the answer, the successor, or the sequel to everything.*[53]

In strange contrast to this economic and technological conservatism was the studio's unique readiness to address the darkest aspects of the Great Depression, thorny social and political topics no other studio dared touch. The studio became associated in the popular imagination with 'social conscience' films with titles like *I Was a Member of a Chain Gang* (1930) and *Public Enemy* (1931).

Jack Warner was a contradictory figure at the heart of a contradictory studio. The youngest and most famous of the brothers, it was he who pioneered this 'cinema of poverty'. A committed Democrat of poor origins, Jack Warner believed in the social value of the studio's dramas of dispossession and redemption. This emphasis on the working class also supplied a profitable hook during the Great Depression, as out-of-work audiences sought comfort in pictures valorising the poor and disenfranchised, cheering not the upwardly mobile Rudolph Valentinos and Buster Keatons, but heroes more in the Charlie Chaplin vein, hobos and nomads and drunks. Beneath Jack Warner's narrative sympathy for the under-classes lurked a genius for exploitation. He so violently opposed labour unionisation that he once turned fire hoses on a picket line of strikers. It was not for nothing that discontented employees nicknamed the studio 'San Quentin' after the most notorious prison in California.

Jack Warner, then 39 years old, had assumed control over production in 1931, a few months before Bette Davis signed on. He was a forceful public personality who never hesitated to spar with even his highest-ranking employees, including Humphrey Bogart, James Cagney and Davis, who together racked up an estimable 20 suspensions in 12 years. In fonder moments, Davis referred to her boss as a sort of surrogate father; in the less fond (and far more frequent) ones, their familial spats made entertainment headlines across the world. Diva and mogul shared many qualities – contempt for authority, vast, flammable ambition and extreme obstinacy – but one important distinction divided them from the beginning. While Bette Davis considered herself a great classical artist, Jack Warner was a committed philistine who held high art in lifelong contempt and took pride in remarks like 'I would rather take a fifty-mile hike than crawl through a book' and 'I prefer to skip the long ones and get a synopsis from the story department.'[54] His profit-orientated worldview permitted no pining for 'quality' and 'high art'.

Davis appeared in eight pictures during her first year at Warners – a colossal, but by no means atypical, output at a studio that prized velocity over polish. She recoiled time and again from the shabby, sub-literate scripts Warner foisted on her, but because her contract contained no 'right of refusal' clause, she had no choice but to carry on sleepwalking through also-ran parts that one critic dismissed in aggregate as 'elaborate piffle'.[55] As her doubts about this no-nonsense, inartistic approach to filmmaking multiplied, Davis prayed for Jack Warner to wake up and take proper advantage of her gifts. She never ceased to hope that the

'I'd love to kiss you, but I just washed my hair,' a platinum publicity still of a sultry Davis from *Cabin in the Cotton* 1932

next role would be 'It', the breakthrough, the definitive proof of her talent.

Her optimism increased with *Cabin in the Cotton*, a clichéd picture even by Warners' standards, distinguished only by her remarkable performance. Davis had great fun playing Madge, the scheming rich girl in a town of poor sharecroppers. She often cited this character's brush-off comment, 'I'd love to kiss you, but I just washed my hair,' as her all-time favourite line of dialogue. Madge was the first *downright, forthright bitch* Davis had ever portrayed on film, and the actress considered the part a *signpost, had the powers that be really thought about it, of the parts I could* really *play*.[56] The powers that be didn't seem to think about it at all. Even as critics cheered the 'flashy, luminous newcomer [who] romps off with first honours', Jack Warner ignored Davis's pleas for more stimulating projects.[57]

Davis made the same steady progress over the next year, appearing in seven pictures between January 1933 and April 1934. And yet, after more than three years in the movies, Davis was beginning to lose patience. Hollywood had failed her on multiple counts. If she was not to be famous or even much respected, she had at least counted on long-term security, but her new wealth had only altered the complexion of her financial hardships. Now she had to bankroll her mother's extravagances and pay for her sister's treatment.

Hollywood had not satisfied one single ambition. She had no name in the marquee lights, no fabulous wealth – not even a knight-in-shining-armour love affair. Of Davis's many schoolgirl crushes during her early years in the movies, not a single prospect materialised. Either she was never quite as seductive as her co-stars, or her mother was too talented a watchdog, or – as with George Cukor's company in Rochester – she was just working too hard for romance.

In early 1932, Davis's sister Bobby, 3000 miles away in Massachusetts, suffered her severest nervous breakdown to date. Ruthie knew that she must tend to her younger daughter on the

In the spring of 1933 – the year that Prohibition was repealed and the New Deal first promulgated, several weeks after the inauguration of Franklin Delano Roosevelt – Bette Davis participated in a cross-country publicity tour, visiting 16 cities in 16 days with Warner Brothers. Though she had by then appeared in more than a dozen movies, the actress still harboured serious reservations about Hollywood, and spoke of cinema as a tawdry haven for second-raters. But on this whistle-stop tour, the up-close evidence of her fans' countrywide devotion showed Davis for the first time 'what films meant to people' and began to persuade her that the future of acting lay not on the velvet-curtained proscenium, but inside the crumbling movie palaces.[58] A great Democrat, she determined to embrace this greatest of democratic arts, or something like that: *In a broken-down country,* she wrote, *Hollywood's stars were America's royalty and their stars the most devoted in the world.*[59]

East Coast, but was reluctant to do so without tying up some loose ends in the Wild West first. Her 23-year-old starlet-daughter must marry, Ruthie decided, while still a virgin.

As luck would have it, Davis's Cushing Academy swain, Harmon (nicknamed 'Ham') Oscar Nelson, had moved to California that same spring to seek his fortunes as a musician. Never one to let a good opportunity slip, Ruthie nominated Nelson emergency groom and, despite her daughter's reservations, dragged the bewildered couple onto the Interstate after an engagement lasting all of two days, heading to Arizona, where marriage licences didn't require the same waiting period as in California. On 18 August 1932, Davis – her resistance weakened by work, Ruthie's carping, and the all-night drive – married her long-lost high-school sweetheart in three-digit heat.

I wore a two-piece beige street dress that resembled the sand of the Arizona desert after the rain it never gets, brown accessories, and two limp gardenia. I kept thinking of the picture I'd always had of myself as a bride – dewy and divine in white satin and orange blossoms, coming up a white-ribboned aisle to the strains of Mendelssohn.[60]

Soon after the wedding, Ruthie towed the ailing Bobby back to Los Angeles with her. There, the two of them set up house with the newlyweds, and posed considerable threats to the Nelsons' domestic harmony. The couple's mismatched work schedules created other stresses. Nelson's orchestra-leader job wound down at dawn just as Davis was rushing off to another 16-hour day at the studio. On the Nelsons' rare evenings alone, Davis, without the luxury of a dress rehearsal, bungled her new role as devoted housewife. Nelson in turn resented playing 'Mr Bette Davis', as he soon became known in the press. As the income gap between husband and wife widened – by 1934, she was making $1000 a week to Nelson's $100 – Nelson prevailed upon Davis to adjust her lifestyle to his income. On his salary, he could scarcely afford rent on the cramped, unfashionable house where he was stuck with

Bette and the first of her four husbands, Harmon Oscar Nelson, driven to the altar by Davis's relentless mother their union did not last long.

Ruthie and Bobby. Resentful of being 'kept', Nelson refused even to discuss moving into a residence better suited to stardom.

Davis later linked her husband's income-insecurities to her decision, in late 1933, to undergo her first abortion. Though Ruthie, obsessed with Davis's destiny as an actress, may have crusaded against motherhood, it was Mildred Rogers who cast the decisive ballot. Mildred was the protagonist of W Somerset Maugham's novel, *Of Human Bondage*. When Davis read the screenplay adaptation of Maugham's novel in the autumn of 1933, she saw in Mildred – a slatternly East End waitress who torments her timid, club-footed admirer – her first shot at greatness in Hollywood. Mildred obsessed Davis like no character since

Hedvig. She had been *born* to play the part, would die if she didn't. Nothing, certainly not childbirth, would stop her.

OF HUMAN BONDAGE AND THE DAVIS STYLE

Before Hollywood, Bette Davis had judged herself 'more striking than beautiful', but she had never questioned her fundamental attractiveness.[61] Her physical idiosyncrasies – the wide-set, bugged eyes, the small features, the diminutiveness of her frame – had always seemed assets, not liabilities. Her mother never tired of photographing her, and as an itinerant teenager with far less money than her peers, Davis had relied on good looks and charisma to sail to popularity. Later, during her first sallies onstage, men had admired, wooed and on occasion even proposed to her. On Broadway writers, directors and critics had united in admiration of her unconventional appearance.

Following an unfortunate misunderstanding on her first after-noon on the West Coast, however, Davis's confidence about her beauty had taken a steady dive. *They didn't know what to do with something that looked like me*, Davis told a talk-show host 40 years later of her arrival in Hollywood in December 1930. *At that age, I want to tell you, in 1930, I was the Yankee-est, most modest virgin who ever walked the earth.*[62] Bedraggled and exhausted after their five-day cross-country journey by train, Bette and Ruthie Davis waited for hours for Universal's publicity man to fetch them, but he never came. The studio later explained that the chaperone had met the train but returned to the studio alone, claiming not to have observed a single passenger who even 'remotely' resembled an actress.[63]

If her tepid welcome to the Hollywood doll's house first dam-aged Davis's self-confidence, her wallflower status at Universal sealed those insecurities for evermore. For the rest of her life, Bette Davis would rage against Nature for denying her the cos-metic ingredients of stardom: the pale blonde hair, the cherry mouth, the endless eyelashes and empty gaze. *Today, I do think I was beautiful*, she told an interviewer in the 1980s. *Then I didn't,*

and I always wanted to look like someone else. That's the entire point about my appearance. Because I was dissatisfied, I was ready to experiment . . . I was very ready to look awful. Or plain or older. I sometimes did my best to look my worst![64]

Davis saw Mildred in *Of Human Bondage* as her first big chance to parade her willingness to *experiment* and to *look awful*. By the time the script hit her doorstep, many actresses had already turned down the part, reluctant

Film historian David Thomson comments on Davis's unconventional looks: 'Her unexpectedness began with the implausibility of a far-from-pretty girl become a movie star. At once hysterically mortified and daring us to admit that she was not attractive, how could the lady with pulsing eyes succeed unless she was a serious actress? This implied that she alone in Hollywood was a real professional; those others, more beautiful and calm, must also be emptier.'[65]

to endanger their pin-up popularity with such a villainous role. These rejections only steeled Davis's resolve. If she was to be barred from that 'list of actresses who are best at playing sweet young things in ruffles', she could achieve something far more rare than beauty: realism.[66]

It was RKO, however, not Warners, who was making *Of Human Bondage*. Davis could not morph into Mildred without Jack Warner's permission to 'loan' her. This permission the mogul steadfastly withheld. Like the rest of Hollywood, Warner considered Mildred a sure route to professional suicide and determined to safeguard her bland next-door-neighbour persona onscreen. When all Davis's sweet-talking and pleading failed her, the actress resorted to old-fashioned harassment. She camped outside her boss's office every day at 7 am until at last Warner, wearied by the only creature whose stubbornness exceeded his own, consented to the loan by borrowing one of Davis's own favourite sayings: 'Go hang yourself, then!'

Ecstatic, Davis hired a Cockney cleaning woman and shadowed her night and day to perfect Mildred's accent. Davis fluttered on to the RKO set confident and prepared, only to meet the open disdain of her co-star Leslie Howard, the upper-class British actor who would later become most famous for his role as Ashley Wilkes in *Gone With the Wind* (1939). Angry that some lower-caste Yank had hijacked a role so explicitly conceived for a Londoner, Howard treated Davis as if she were trying to destroy his vehicle.

Davis retaliated in her performance, sparing no detail in her metamorphosis into a low-class, manipulative Cockney slut, and from the first day of filming Howard began to fear that, if the upstart American did not ruin his film, she just might steal it. In the film, Howard played Philip Carey, a pathetic limping romantic who has recently traded his dream of becoming an artist for a sensible future as a doctor. Despite her unmistakeable crudeness Philip falls hard for Mildred, who alternately teases and torments him, proclaiming that in no circumstances could she ever be interested in a cripple. Her resolve weakens only when her favoured lover impregnates, then abandons her, whereupon she allows Philip to support her – but only until something better comes along. Philip's unrelenting obsession with Mildred survives all betrayals, even as it threatens to destroy first his possessions, and then his sanity.

The opening of the film, in the summer of 1934, confirmed Howard's fears. Reviewers all but ignored his performance to marvel at the powerhouse playing Mildred. *Life* magazine went so far as to salute Davis for 'probably the greatest performance ever recorded on screen by a US actress'.[67] Against a backdrop of sequins and cheesecake grins, Davis blazed into the public eye as a force of nature, a panting virago, a combustible beast. 'Bette Davis would probably have been burned as a witch if she had lived two or three hundred years ago,' one critic wrote, expressing the intermingled awe and repulsion in most audiences.[68] 'She gives the curious feeling of being charged with power which can find no ordinary outlet,' observed another critic.[69]

If portraying a larger-than-life monster necessarily excludes all subtlety or restraint, Davis was lucky in never having prized either attribute. From her first slack-jawed sneer, well past Mildred's pulse-stopping climactic monologue (the famous speech that ends with 'After you kissed me I always used to wipe my mouth – *wipe my mouth!*'), Davis flaunts her fearlessness as a performer, her readiness to court dislike, even disgust, in the interests of dramatic punch.

The exaggerated nastiness of Mildred's character authorised Davis's tendency, so long suppressed, to externalise personality, to let appearance mirror soul. Mildred is an evil creature and evil, Davis believed, breeds ugliness. She vetoed the director's advice and applied her own make-up for the final scenes of the film, in which Mildred wastes away with consumption. Too responsible a performer to *die of a dread disease looking as if a deb had missed her noon nap,* Davis showed Mildred's moral defects in her appearance.[70] The result – black circles under her eyes, drool at her lips, electric-socket hair – supplied extraordinary proof of valuing authenticity over beauty. What Davis – never a rigorous realist – defined as honest and accurate, some judged simply grotesque. Even so, in 1934, at a time when Mae West's eyebrow-raising innuendoes marked the limit of female boldness on film, Davis was revolutionary. Before *Of Human Bondage*, no actress had ever dared, much less chosen, to look ugly on camera. So even if Graham Greene, in his review of *Of Human Bondage,* detected in Davis's 'precise nervy voice, the pale ash-blond hair, the popping neurotic eyes, a kind of corrupt and phosphorescent prettiness', the actress wanted no movie-goer to forget that prettiness had never been her intent.[71]

Mildred was the long-awaited turning point in Davis's

Hollywood journey. Though *Of Human Bondage* was her 22nd film, most critics commended Davis as a 'newcomer' to the screen. *We have such reverence for the chance that {Of Human Bondage} gave my fast-disappearing career*, Davis told *Film Weekly* in 1935, *that everything in our family dates B.B. (Before Bondage) and A.B.*[72] Indeed, the film altered not just Davis's career, but also Hollywood's conceptions of women. Her rendering of the first anti-heroine in Hollywood history remains arresting today; it encapsulates her strengths as a performer even as it anticipates her excesses.

Mildred Rogers altered not only Bette Davis's career, but also the history of the Academy Awards. To ensure that no such controversies undermined the Award's status again, the Academy moved to standardise the nomination and voting process, and in 1937 took the further step of engaging the accounting firm of Price Waterhouse (now PriceWaterhouseCoopers) to count the ballots, an arrangement still in effect today. Davis left another, more personal imprint on the Academy Awards, though many contest this legacy: the name 'Oscar'. She claimed to be so struck by the resemblance of the shapely statuette's backside to that of her husband, Harmon Oscar Nelson, that she nicknamed it after him.

When the Academy of Motion Picture Arts and Sciences left Davis's name off the list of 1935's Best Actress nominees, fans around the world, recognising the historical significance of her performance, roared in protest. Davis openly blamed Jack Warner for blocking the nomination, but it's more likely that Mildred had, quite simply, baffled the conservative Academy, which was still an embryonic institution in the early 1930s. While the write-in campaign initiated on her behalf failed, Davis never doubted that the scandal had brought her far more press than any statuette.

A year after the controversy, at the 1936 Academy Awards ceremony, Davis felt amply compensated when the famous director D W Griffith named her Best Actress for her estimable, but by no means explosive, performance in *Dangerous*, in which Davis played

Davis accepts the first of her Oscars at the 1936 Academy Awards ceremony for her performance in *Dangerous*

Joyce Heath, a washed-up ex-Broadway star doomed to jinx all the men in her life. Walking to the stage to accept her trophy, Davis pleaded astonishment, and in her spotted housedress she certainly looked unprepared for the honour. Ruthie Davis excused the low-rent outfit as her daughter's 'way, possibly unconsciously, of telling the Academy it wasn't all that important in her scheme of things'.[73] Davis echoed this indifference in an offhand comment to reporters that night: *I don't take the movies seriously and anyone who does is in for a headache.*[74] If the blasé posture fooled few, the frumpiness reinforced the message Mildred had so unmistakeably

Elizabeth I as a sort of 'female Frankenstein', uncomfortably it was not only her studio but also her co-star Errol Flynn, who held this view of Davis in *The Private Lives of Elizabeth and Essex* 1939

delivered the year before: Bette Davis was a Serious Actress – less symmetrical and glossy than her peers, but infinitely more talented, more intelligent and more authentic.

Whether insecure or ideological in origin, Davis's willingness to experiment with her appearance evolved into the touchstone of her art. Whenever possible, she repudiated the Dream Factory's skin-deep priorities in defence of her own loftier capabilities: *I always looked the way my character should look – ugly or pretty, I certainly didn't waste time trying to be a little glamourpuss.*[75] After Mildred, Davis routinely overrode her directors' aesthetic decisions about her appearance. In 1937, in the gangster picture *Marked Woman*, to indicate the brutal beating that her character suffered, the make-up department placed one decorative bandage on her forehead. Annoyed that she resembled more a nun than a patient, Davis left the set during her lunch break, hoping to consult her doctor about a more medically plausible approach. An hour later, she drove back on to the lot covered in scrapes, her cheeks so puffed and bruised that the watchman called ahead to warn the crew that their star had been in a car wreck.

In the 1939 film *The Old Maid*, over the course of which her character ages 20 years, Davis drew out the disappointments of her character's spinster existence in the dullness of her complexion and the tightness of her bun – a stark contrast to her co-star Miriam Hopkins, as fresh-faced and glimmering in the last frame as in the first. That same year Davis, then 30, was cast as the ageing Queen Elizabeth I in *The Private Lives of Elizabeth and Essex*. After studying Holbein's portrait of the ageing monarch, Davis declared their resemblance too *amazing* for a difference of three decades to conceal, never mind if the studio regarded the queen who emerged as a sort of 'female Frankenstein'[76].

The Star System · 1935–1939

I miss motion picture executives like Jack Warner, Louis B Mayer and Darryl Zanuck, Bette Davis said in 1984. *They were gamblers. They gave us all a chance. They gave me a career.*[77] A half-century earlier, upon completing her role in *Of Human Bondage* at RKO, Davis expressed no such fondness. The same week that she finished *Of Human Bondage*, Davis learned that her father in Boston had suffered a minor heart attack. Upset by this news and steeled by Mildred's fierce example, Davis aired her dissatisfaction with Warners in public for the first time when she rejected the part of Perry Mason's secretary-sidekick in *The Case of the Howling Dog.*

Warner responded by suspending her: no holiday in disguise, that punishment, as moguls could tack periods of unpaid suspension on to an actor's existing contract, thereby lengthening its run. This time Davis got off easily, if only because *Of Human Bondage* hit the screens just two weeks into her sentence. Jack Warner – not a man to let a suddenly valuable property depreciate – put Davis back to work. But her reprieve left Davis's contractual situation unchanged. Like other members of the studio system, from the stars to the screenwriters to the sound technicians, Davis worked under a rigid, seven-year contract, a system that granted complete security but no liberty. She was paid a fixed weekly salary, and had little say over the publicity generated in her name, or the directors who made her films. She had no 'right of refusal' clause: no power to choose among the mostly shabby scripts Warner foisted on her.

As ever-larger audiences recognised her name, Davis objected more and more to the abuses Warner heaped on what was, after all, her only logo: *Even when I knew a script was crap, I did my best and expected everyone else to – because it was my name above the title, and the supporting cast never gets blamed, but the star always does, especially a woman star.*[78] Warners' laziness not only offended her refined sensibilities, it threatened her public identity too – for Bette Davis, the only one that counted.

She could do no more than gripe, for the studio heads exercised absolute control over every aspect of film production, from writing and shooting to distribution and exhibition. The Supreme Court would later find this system of vertical integration to be in violation of competition law, but during the Great Depression of the 1930s, with the New Deal government teaming up with big business, this 'oligopoly' ensured the survival of the studios and provided their only means of producing around 52 films a year on tiny budgets.

The tycoons' chief creative involvement in this business consisted of spotting, and rapidly indenturing, talent. They remade their discoveries, altered their names and rewrote their biographies. The moguls recognised the financial advantages of the star system early on. Audience loyalties congealed around specific performers (and, by extension, studios) more even than sequels and adaptations of bestselling novels, so stars reduced production risks by attracting a loyal movie-goer in a predictable market. As high-ranking stars became the economic cornerstone of the studio system, the most popular actors (or, in 'mogulese', the most reliable commodities) shouldered a crushing workload. 'The star system in the 1930s gradually took on the reality, if not the appearance, of a star serfdom,' film critic Alexander Walker writes. 'Glamour was its camouflage and fame its dazzling illusion. But behind the grandeur of being a movie star in these years lay all the gradations of servitude.'[79]

There are certain times that I wish that I'd taken a breather, Bette Davis remarked toward the end of her life, *but in those days when I was building a career, I couldn't, or I'd have got lost in the shuffle. The way you made the public notice you then was to make three or four pictures a year – each totally different. Studios understood that, even before actors did.*[80]

Davis felt her old optimism surge when, directly after her row with Jack Warner over *Of Human Bondage*, he assigned her two good pictures in a row. As a deranged housewife in the Paul Muni vehicle *Bordertown*, Davis savoured every twitch of her onscreen nervous breakdown. But then, after another gratifying role in the nouveau-Cinderella melodrama, *The Girl from Tenth Avenue*, Jack Warner saddled Davis with two projects as pathetic as any she had ever played.

Before she had a chance to protest again, *Dangerous* came along, and with it, Davis's first Academy Award – the trophy that changed everything. *Dangerous* was a trifle of a film, and Davis's role as an alcoholic ex-stage-star less than extraordinary, but the trophy demonstrated that, after the controversy over *Of Human Bondage,* her leverage in the industry had stuck; the Oscar formalised her status as one of Hollywood's talents on the rise. The first Warners actress ever accorded such an honour, Davis seized on her Oscar as the bargaining chip in her never-ending struggle for creative autonomy. Warner rewarded Davis with a sympathetic part as a besotted provincial girl in *The Petrified Forest*, the celebrated gangster picture that introduced Humphrey Bogart (1899–1957) to the screen. ('Even when I was carrying a gun,' Bogart said of his co-star, 'she scared the bejesus out of me.')[81] Davis was still taking comfort from this high-quality project – the film that *made Bogie's career and didn't hurt mine* – when Warner, as if to check her hubris, dumped another pair of monstrosities on her, *The Golden Arrow* and *Satan Met a Lady*, the latter an inept version of *The Maltese Falcon*.[82] Davis erupted. 'Just be a good girl,' Warner soothed her, 'and everything will work out.' Bette Davis did the opposite, and went on strike.[83]

Davis with Leslie Howard and Humphrey Bogart in *The Petrified Forest* of 1935 it was this film that introduced Bogart to the screen

Davis had many sympathisers in the industry, colleagues tired of the moguls' ever-tightening grips on their careers. The formation of the Screen Actors Guild in 1933 represented one of the stars' first unified efforts to contest this treatment, and by the late 1930s, feuds between studios and actors – such as Katharine Hepburn at RKO and Carole Lombard at Paramount – had become a matter of course. Change was coming in other directions as well. In 1939, David O Selznick's *Gone With the Wind*, the first independently produced blockbuster in Hollywood history, demonstrated that if producers could make pictures without contract players, players might also make pictures without contracts. Over the next few years, the World War Two boom in cinema attendance strengthened solo entrepreneurs like Selznick. The star system decomposed even faster after 1943, when Olivia de Havilland won a historic contract case against Warners. Finding the studio guilty of inflicting 'virtual peonage' and a 'life of bondage' on its employees, the Los Angeles Supreme Court ordered Warners to release de Havilland at the original expiry date of her contract, rather than forcing her to stay on to cover all her periods of suspension.[84] This ruling drastically undermined the studios' right to lock actors into long-term contracts, and the next several years saw many similar challenges upheld.

Change was imminent, but in 1935 the moguls still ruled like feudal lords. Believing that Bette Davis was indebted to her studio not just for her success but for her very existence in Hollywood, Jack Warner disciplined her like a spoiled adolescent, grounding her and freezing her allowance. He also leaked to the press that Davis's complaints were solely motivated by money: $5,000 a week, apparently, did not suffice to feed and clothe a Tinseltown princess. That her actual wage was less than a third of this figure earned her little popular sympathy during the Great Depression, when most Americans considered even a two-figure salary a king's ransom.

In her arguments with Warner, Davis never failed to mention how much money her recent pictures had made for the studio, a rising scale from $400,000 to $800,000. In public, however, because she knew that she had a PR problem on her hands, Davis insisted, not entirely without justice, that money had no bearing on her misery. To prove it, she rejected Warner's proposed payrise, which required her to extend her contract for another two years. She would compromise, she said, only if he addressed her central demands: the right to choose her own scripts and a limit of four pictures a year, both all but unheard-of privileges in the studio era. The two sides had reached deadlock and certain practical considerations began to weaken Davis's resolve. She had an expensive family to support: a sister who required frequent hospitalisations and a mother who required ever higher credit limits. These burdens looked set to doom Davis's dispute to the usual pattern – a long suspension, loss of income, the performer indebted and desperate, ending in a settlement that favoured the studio – when a foreign interloper appeared. Ludovico Toeplitz, an Italian producer based in England, offered Davis $50,000, equivalent to almost a year's salary at Warners, to make a single film with his company.

The sum decided Davis. Under cover of night, the 28-year-old actress, who had never before travelled outside of America, absconded with her semi-estranged husband to Canada, and there boarded a ship for Scotland. Following an ambitious stab at a second honeymoon touring the birthplace of her father's ancestors in Wales, Davis settled into the Savoy Hotel in London for pre-liminary negotiations with Toeplitz. She professed surprise at Fleet Street's rabid interest in her case – she had no idea that her fame stretched across the Atlantic.

So boosted was she by her unexpected status as international superstar that Davis took the arrival of Jack Warner, who had pur-sued his ill-mannered chattel across the ocean, in her stride. When she refused to listen to reason, Warner engaged Sir Patrick Hastings, one of Britain's most eminent barristers (later Agatha Christie's model for the protagonist of *Witness for the Prosecution*) and prepared to take Davis to court. Davis hastened to secure equally prestigious representation, but was floored when her counsel, Sir William Jowitt, demanded a retainer of £10,000 – an impossible figure after months of unpaid suspension. Before she succeeded in persuading Jowitt to add this sum to her bill, Davis consulted her husband for fund-raising suggestions, only to dis-cover that Nelson was planning to sail to Manhattan, where he had landed a gig as bandleader. Despite Davis's vociferous oppo-sition, Nelson left England days before her trial.

The couple did not divorce for another two years, but Nelson's departure from London marks the *de facto* end of Davis's first marriage. The actress called it quits then and there, but it was Nelson who finally filed for divorce in late 1938, a time when husbands almost never appeared as plaintiffs in such suits. Citing grounds of 'cruel and inhuman treatment', Nelson alleged that Davis, who regularly studied scripts in bed, was 'so engrossed in her profession that she . . . neglected and failed to perform her duties as a wife'.[85]

The actress wore the same simple business suit to court every day in the hopes of discrediting Warner's smears, but no sartorial prudence could defuse the impact of Hastings's opening argument. 'I think, m'lord,' he began, 'that this is the action of a very naughty young lady, and what she really wants is more money.' Hastings followed with similarly sexist and patronising jabs that did little to improve the actress's image. 'Miss Davis has characterised her employment at Warner Bros as "slavery". But the "slavery" had a silver lining because the "slave" was, to say the least, well-remunerated.'[86] Sneering aside, Hastings anchored his argument in the basic legal definition of a contract. However draconian the document's provisions, the actress had read it, she had signed it, and she was now violating it.

As the journalists' sympathies slid from slave to master, Davis's counsel Sir William Jowitt decided not to allow his client to appear on the stand. In place of live theatrics, Jowitt cited a letter Davis had written Warner earlier that year: *As a happy person I can work like Hell – as an unhappy one I make myself and everyone around me unhappy.*[87] The self-analysis would prove more true than anyone predicted, but the court deemed it irrelevant. Jowitt brought his already wishy-washy defence to its conclusion by blundering into rather unfortunate rhetoric: 'This contract is so strict that Miss Davis could not become a waitress in a restaurant or an assistant in a hairdresser's shop in the wilds of Africa – whether for love or money.'[88]

The judge announced his decision in favour of the studio on 19 October 1936. Although Jack Warner could not 'compel' the actress to work for him, her contract expressly forbade her to work elsewhere for its duration. Davis faced an excruciatingly simple choice: either return to Warners or remain unemployed for another 36 months.

Proclaiming herself a scapegoat, the victim of Britons' ancestral hatred for Americans, Davis fled to a tiny seaside cottage near Brighton, where she contemplated appealing the decision. She had $15,000 of legal expenses and was set to lose an additional $1,600 for every week of suspension. Soon after Davis cabled her mother in California for guidance, an unexpected caller paid her a visit: George Arliss, the English actor who had introduced Davis into the Warner family five years earlier. 'Either you work in California,' Arliss advised, 'or you never work in this industry again.'[89]

Grudgingly, Davis chose work. *When I was a young thing and not very wise*, the actress told reporters at the dock in New York, *I signed the contract which ties me up until 1942. I'll be an old woman by 1942, but I'm going back . . . And all I can say is, the hell with it.*[90] By 1942, Bette Davis was the highest paid woman in America.

THE REWARD
It is a curious footnote to Hollywood history that most remember Bette Davis's 1936 court defeat as a victory. *I lost the battle*, the actress later claimed, *but I won the war.*[91] Sloping back to Hollywood in late 1936, Davis was resigned to *serve five years in the Warner jail*[92] but she was pleasantly surprised to find that her prestige and leverage had grown tenfold during her absence. Instead of bullying his prodigal player, Jack Warner lavished unprecedented kindnesses and privileges on Davis. Not only did he agree to subtract her legal debt from her pay in reasonable increments, he even volunteered to raise her wage to $2,000 a

week. While Davis later recognised this pay-rise as a trap to tighten the studio's hold on her, at the time the cash relieved her most pressing difficulties.

Even without the money, Davis's proof of success lay in the quality of the scripts that Warner was offering her: they were, all of a sudden, *star vehicles*. It had taken an ocean and a trial, but Davis had finally won her chief's respect.

In *Marked Woman*, her first post-trial assignment, Davis starred as Mary Dwight, a nightclub 'hostess' who takes her gangster-keepers to court after her younger sister is murdered – a role that solidified Davis's reputation as a brazen, fearless woman willing to do battle for her principles, especially because Mary Dwight, unlike the actress playing her, defeats her oppressors and vindicates her profession. Perhaps this legal coup on film prompted the

'Even when I was carrying a gun, she scared the bejesus out of me,' said Bogart of his co-star. Davis, Bogart and Edward G Robinson in *Kid Galahad* 1936

popular revision of Davis's court case – or perhaps it was just the overnight explosion of the actress's popularity.

In her next assignment, *Kid Galahad,* Davis played a gangster's moll opposite Edward G Robinson. As in *The Petrified Forest,* Davis's winning role in this prestigious prize-fighter film – what Davis described as a textbook example of a *man's picture* – introduced her to larger audiences than ever before.[93] Her two subsequent pictures, *That Certain Woman* with Henry Fonda and *It's Love I'm After* with Leslie Howard, further consolidated Davis's appeal to the public and prominence in the press. (They also, not unimportantly, grossed one million dollars each.)

Then, in the summer of 1937, only four movies after her reluctant homecoming, Davis declined to report on the set of *The Hollywood Hotel*. Certain that the actress's only ailment was disapproval of the film's dim script, Jack Warner slapped another suspension on her. But this time, it seemed, Davis wasn't playacting. She spent the entire summer in bed, where her nursemaid and secretary Ruthie, a recent convert to Christian Science, harassed her by reading aloud from Mary Baker Eddy's *Science and Health with Key to the Scriptures*.

Davis only rose from her sickbed to meet William Wyler, whom Jack Warner had borrowed from Samuel Goldwyn to direct *Jezebel*, an extremely old-fashioned morality tale that Jack Warner had purchased to console Davis for losing the part of Scarlett in *Gone With the Wind*. *Jezebel* centred on a bitchy Southern belle character remarkably similar to Scarlett O'Hara: Julie Marsden, a spoiled New Orleans heiress who spurns custom by wearing a scandalous red gown to a society ball. Far from tolerating her joke, Julie's fiancé Preston (played by Henry Fonda) forces her to dance with him, on and on and on, even as the glaring scions of *haute* New Orleans banish her from their favour for ever.

Jezebel had been a hugely popular play starring Davis's once-and-future nemesis Miriam Hopkins, who had treated Davis so shabbily when they worked together in Rochester. Because Hollywood producers doubted that audiences would warm to the egocentric, bratty protagonist, the screen adaptation was delayed again and again. It was only the resurgence of popular interest in all things antebellum spurred by the publication of *Gone With the Wind* that convinced Warner to invest in the picture. Intent on beating Margaret Mitchell's bestselling novel to the cinemas, Warner poured more money into *Jezebel* than into any previous Bette Davis vehicle, presenting her with a script of unsurpassed quality and a director of unsurpassed talent. A perfectionist notorious for demanding long takes (thus placing a greater burden on the actors' performances) and incessant retakes, William 'Forty-Take' Wyler believed that no director had ever properly captured Davis onscreen before. He vowed to be the first, at any cost.

Davis spoke of her exclusion from *Gone With the Wind* as the greatest regret of her career. *I was as perfect for Scarlett as Clark Gable was for Rhett*, she insisted, but the film's producers agreed that Davis lacked the necessary physical magnetism to make Rhett Butler's pursuit of Scarlett believable.[91] Among Davis's other missed-role regrets, only turning down the role of Blanche DuBois in *A Streetcar Named Desire* and the Oscar-winning lead in *Come Back, Little Sheba* and losing Martha in *Who's Afraid of Virginia Woolf?* to Elizabeth Taylor, came close to missing Scarlett.

Davis so fed on this fastidiousness that she fell in love with Wyler during the making of *Jezebel*. Though bereft of animal attractions (the squat director was known as 'the Golem'), Wyler had seduced many leading ladies with his charismatic and commanding personality. Typically, Davis judged her affair with Wyler (she was still married to Nelson at the time) to be different, the ultimate affair, and flaunted her extramarital liaison until everyone in Hollywood knew about it except her husband. As the on-set romance heated up, frugal Jack Warner began objecting to the innumerable delays besetting the production. (Fonda, whose wife was pregnant, wrig-

Jezebel was Davis's consolation prize for losing the role of Scarlett O'Hara to Vivien Leigh. The lavish antebellum drama trumped its rival, *Gone with the Wind*, at the box-office and sealed Davis's superstardom.

gled with impatience for better reason. Promised that the shooting would wrap before Christmas of 1937, Fonda began to doubt that he would reach New York in time for the birth of his first child, Jane.)

The shooting was finally winding to a close when, on New Year's Day of 1938, 54-year-old Harlow Morrell Davis had another heart attack, this one fatal. Davis was crushed, for with her father died the possibility of coming to terms with her past. At the time, however, her work-obsessions prevailed over personal considerations: Davis was so intent on finishing *Jezebel* that she decided not to attend her father's funeral in Boston. Days later, studio doctors informed the actress that she was pregnant for the second time. Davis knew that the baby belonged to Wyler, but not even true love could blind her to the dictates of stardom, and she underwent her second abortion without hesitation. If she had no time to make a cameo at her father's funeral, she must surely deny herself the luxury of playing mommy for the next 40 years.

In spite of these setbacks, *Jezebel* beat *Gone With the Wind* to the cinema. It raked in more than $1.5 million in profits and, more importantly, putting its star in a *different category as a performer*.[95] Critics and audiences alike recognised that only Bette Davis could have played the famous red-dress scene with such élan. And, true to his intentions, William Wyler had captured the full range of Davis's talent onscreen as no one had before, authenticating one of the actress's favourite theatre sayings: *You're only as good as your director*.

Jezebel clinched Bette Davis's superstardom for good. The first proof of her fame came when former Communist James Matthews testified before the House Un-American Activities Committee and accused Bette Davis, among other Hollywood actors, of covertly serving Communist interests against the US government. The FBI opened a file on Davis – an honour seldom associated with some nameless chorus girl. Nothing came of the suspicions, but Washington kept a close eye on Davis through the early 1950s. Davis also appeared on the cover of *Time* magazine that summer of 1938, but more thrilling still was the new contract she signed stipulating a weekly wage of $3,500 and releasing her from all remaining legal debts. Davis was so overjoyed by this pay-rise that she failed to notice that she had been granted no

Of her many affairs Davis's brief dalliance with Howard Hughes excited the gossip columnists to the greatest pitch

more creative autonomy – the stated goal of her 1936 suit – than in her previous contract.

Though she later crowned Wyler the one true love of her life, Davis rebounded with great resilience after he left her in January 1938, less than a month after *Jezebel* wrapped. Later that year, Davis's marriage fell apart for good and, having enjoyed her first taste of adultery with Wyler, she broke loose. Over the next few years Davis hopped from one liaison to the next: with a publicity man at Warners, with the married director of her project immediately following *Jezebel*, *The Sisters*, and, most headline-worthy of all, with Howard Hughes, the billionaire producer, aviator and bisexual known for his dalliances with *le tout* Hollywood. The third time she became pregnant, in 1940, she could offer only vague guesses as to paternity. Her rigid Puritanical upbringing was soon lost in a mess of abortions, affairs and blackmail. In the years of her rapid rise to fame, Bette Davis's personal life featured

Davis's flair for exaggerating the details of her romantic escapades developed as rapidly as her taste for adultery. A few months after Nelson divorced her, Davis – stung by the public humiliation – began relating a farcical episode from the time of her marriage, in which Nelson, suspecting infidelity, sneaked into Howard Hughes's mansion and bugged it. According to Davis, the disgruntled Nelson made a tape of Hughes in bed with Davis, which he then used to blackmail the billionaire for $70,000.

all the implausible incident of one of her early B-movies at Warners.

THE QUEEN OF HOLLYWOOD

In the year 1939, Bette Davis said, *I secured my career and my stardom forever.*[96] For once, she was not exaggerating. The greatest year of Hollywood's Golden Age – the year of *Gone With the Wind, The Wizard of Oz, Stagecoach, Mr Smith Goes to Washington, Ninotchka, The Women* and *Beau Geste* – coincided exactly with the pinnacle of Bette Davis's fame. Even if she had never made another movie, Davis's 1939 films secured her a permanent place in the Hollywood pantheon.

Davis gets the full blast of all the glamour George Hurrell can create in this publicity still for *Dark Victory.* 1939

In February of 1939, she accepted her second Best Actress Academy Award for *Jezebel* – an auspicious beginning to the best of all years. At this ceremony, she dressed the part of the star that by then she indisputably was. Riding on the success of this picture, Davis steamrollered Jack Warner's reservations about *Dark Victory*, a multi-Kleenex tearjerker about Judith Traherne, a carefree playgirl whose trivial, worldly preoccupations vanish when she is diagnosed with a terminal illness. The stage version of *Dark Victory* had been a disaster, despite having the actress Tallulah Bankhead (1903–1968) – one of the most notorious personalities of the century in America – in the starring role. Warner shunned the script's downbeat subject matter, asking, 'Who's going to want to see a picture about a dame who goes blind and dies?'[97]

Perhaps Warner also wondered at Davis's enthusiasm for the script, which was a far cry from Ibsen. Touted in ad copy as 'the greatest picture of a woman's love that the world has ever seen', *Dark Victory* is a hugely sentimental – and not a hugely intelligent – story. But, for Bette Davis, Judith Traherne, like Hedvig and Mildred, represented an unmissable chance to writhe centrestage. It wasn't the size of the part or the number of lines that preoccupied her. In 1935, for example, Davis had been quite happy to take a supporting role in the Paul Muni vehicle *Bordertown*, since her mentally unsound character gets to enjoy a brief but magnificent nervous breakdown scene toward the end of the film. That same year, Davis had objected vigorously to a much larger – and immeasurably more boring – role as a perky girl reporter in *Front Page Woman*.

To vent the peculiar hysteria of her personality, Bette Davis had developed an extremely physical, mannerism-based style of acting, one that flourished only in emotionally overwrought roles. As *Dark Victory* proved, Davis judged a script less by the quality of its writing than by its potential to show off this style. 'Miss Davis needed her bad scripts as sorely as they needed her; they

Davis with matinee idol George Brent in *Dark Victory*. Her role as the tragic Judith Traherne in the intense melodrama turned the film into a runaway hit

were what she needed to wrestle through in that pursuit of "truth" and "realism" [which] to her are always "more than natural,'" Brigid Brophy wrote in a 1962 review of Davis's autobiography, which goes on to compare the actress's hysteria to that of St Teresa. 'For in Miss Davis, control is always chasing after the fantasy, insight after melodrama. The chase creates . . . a wonderful spiral of intensity.'[98]

For Davis, intensity, not high art or self-invention, and certainly not redemption, was the endpoint of acting. Her naturalism resided only in the extremities of human experience. She thrived not in muted slow-burners, as studio executives had often assumed during her long apprenticeship at Universal and Warners, but in scorching love-and-death vehicles. Her preferred roles were heightened embodiments of human vices and virtues: Hedvig represented innocence, Mildred lechery, Julie Marsden vanity. With the aristocratic Judith Traherne, uncomplainingly surrendering to Death, Davis could impersonate Christ in fashionable Long Island equestrian garb.

Released in early 1939, *Dark Victory* was a massive hit, thanks in part to its strong cast, which included Humphrey Bogart and, as one of Judith's beaux, the strapping 27-year-old Ronald Reagan (who had arrived in Hollywood only 18 months before). Jack Warner, however, gave Davis full credit for the film's success, and not simply because of the publicity around the affair she was conducting with her co-star, the glossy matinee idol George Brent, at the time of its release. As Davis had reckoned from the first read-through, Judith Traherne would become one of her best-loved roles, rivalled only by Charlotte Vale in *Now, Voyager* and Margo Channing in *All About Eve*.

'Miss Davis is superb,' raved the *New York Times*. 'More than that, she is enchanted and enchanting. Admittedly it is a great role – rangy, full-bodied, designed for a virtuosa, almost sure to invite the faint damning of "tour de force". But that must not detract from the eloquence, the tenderness, the heart-breaking sincerity with which she has played it. We do not belittle an actress to remark upon her great opportunity; what matters is that she made the utmost of it.'[99] Critics agreed that the beguiling performance put the 31-year-old actress safely in line for her second Academy Award in a row. Though *Gone With the Wind* soon thwarted that possibility, *Dark Victory* remained of lasting importance in Hollywood history as a precursor of the 'women's picture', the genre that would dominate American cinema during World War Two.

Less than a month after *Dark Victory*, Davis appeared in a smaller, but no less sensational, capacity in the historical drama *Juarez*, a loose retelling of Benito Juarez's rebellion against the Austrian Archduke Maximilian, Mexico's weak emperor installed by Napoleon III. Though Paul Muni, the star of the film, campaigned to reduce Davis's already minor role as the Archduke's wife Carlotta, the actress still managed to upstage Muni hands down in her descent-into-madness scene, hands down 'the most unforgettable moment in the picture' and another great example of Davis's conflation of intensity with what she had previously described as 'authenticity'.[100] Or, as Pauline Kael summed up the bravura scene: 'Both frail and tempestuous, she gets a chance to show off her best violent spasms.'[101]

Davis's next picture, *The Old Maid*, would go on to become her biggest money-maker to date when it was released in the summer of 1939. But as her popularity grew, so did the behind-the-scenes strife, in this case between Davis and her haughty, scheming co-star Miriam Hopkins. For the brief time that they had worked under George Cukor in Rochester, Davis had struggled to understand Hopkins's extreme hostility toward her: in 1928, after all, Davis had only been a mousy and somewhat uppity ingénue, and Hopkins the undisputed star of the company. In the decade since Rochester, however, Davis had rocketed to stardom while Hopkins's own career – the one that had once shown so much more promise – had stagnated. The star of *Jezebel* on Broadway, Hopkins especially despised her co-star for having stolen the role of Julie Marsden from her, and – worse yet – winning an Oscar for it. (Less irritating was Davis's 1938 fling with Anatole Livtak, Hopkins's then husband.) Vengeful and immature, Hopkins terrorised her co-star throughout the shooting of *The Old Maid*. *Miss Hopkins appeared on the set of the Old Maid wearing my dress from Jezebel*, Davis seethed many years later. *Oh, she was a swine.*[102]

Seeing the potential in the screenplay, adapted from an Edith Wharton novella, Davis, somewhat uncharacteristically, resolved to parry Hopkins's malice with sweetness. Playing a kindly spinster dedicated to raising the illegitimate child whom Hopkins's more colourful character has taken from her, Davis delivered a sensitive and controlled performance. Hopkins, discomfited by this unexpected mildness, overplayed her part egregiously. It was only when critics omitted her from their reviews and focused exclusively on Davis that Hopkins understood how cleverly she had been upstaged.

Just a week after finishing work on *The Old Maid*, Davis launched into the only Technicolor film she would ever make at Warners, *The Private Lives of Elizabeth and Essex*. For her second picture in a row, on-set altercations marred the production, this time between Davis and the celebrated male beauty Errol Flynn. During filming of *The Old Maid*, jealous Hopkins was mostly to blame for the conflict; *Elizabeth and Essex* was a different story altogether.

The trouble started when Errol Flynn, whose voracious sexual appetite was well known, made no secret of finding Davis exceptionally unattractive (particularly in her plucked and powdered Royal incarnation). Sexual insecurities inflamed, Davis set about maligning Flynn – *that beautiful ass* – as unserious and lazy to anyone who cared to listen; these efforts by no means softened the actor's opinion of her.[103] Luckily, her character, the ageing Queen, felt similar anxieties about her much younger lover, played by Flynn, so the behind-the-scenes tensions translated well on to film. At the time, popular approval of Davis's 'strong, resolute, glamour-skimping characterisation against which Mr Flynn's Essex has about as much chance as a beanshooter against a tank' excused Davis's unprofessional antics.[104]

Bette Davis, Errol Flynn later remarked, 'thought that she was the greatest actress that ever lived', and indeed by the close of 1939, resting on a mantle of four unanimously acclaimed performances, Davis saw little to contest the claim. Nationwide opinion polls in 1940 crowned the celluloid Queen of England the Queen of Hollywood, but even divine right has its downside. After making six pictures in rapid succession, Davis was beginning to feel overworked and under-appreciated. *I was overfull of acting,* she explained. *I was gorged with it, surfeited with it, exhausted with it.*[105] Unwilling to reduce the number of pictures she was expected to make in a year – especially as her box-office returns soared with every project – Warner answered Davis's request for a holiday with another suspension.

As during her previous punishment, Davis took to her bed, this time sinking into a torpor that bore an alarming resemblance to Bobby's periodic depressions. Fearful lest these debilitating fits prove a family legacy, Davis fled to Boston, hoping that her home-town would restore her. But her former high school friends treated Davis – no longer the poor girl in the lunch line – with such exaggerated deference that she soon retreated into a remote corner of New Hampshire. It was in this bucolic setting that she met Arthur Farnsworth, the 31-year-old assistant manager of the inn where she was staying. Rugged and handsome, an amateur pilot and gifted musician, Farnsworth also moonlighted as the entertainer of the many single women passing through the hotel, and wasted no time in seducing the inn's most famous guest. His attentions so absorbed Davis that soon she was refusing all incoming phone calls.

As his highest-grossing star's leave of absence extended into its third month, Warner began to panic until finally he acceded to Davis's request for an annual limit of three pictures. He also increased her salary and vacation days, still without even acknowl-edging her 1936 demands for script and cinematographic approval – the conditions she had always said were central. Davis seemed too pleased with the battles she had won – or too happy re-decorating the 150-year-old farmhouse that she had purchased – to quibble. She was so preoccupied with details of interior design, in fact, that she decided not to return to Los Angeles for the birth of her sister's first child that summer.

After reluctantly leaving New Hampshire that September to tackle another period picture, *All This and Heaven, Too*, Davis came home to mountainous heaps of bills. Ruthie had once again ignored the financial effects of her daughter's long suspension. More disturbing was Bobby's post-partum condition. Childbirth, it seemed, had undone years of relative stability, and Bobby had checked back into hospital with depression. Guilt-ridden Davis had no choice but to invite her sister's socialite husband Robert Pelgram and baby daughter Fay into her household. With a profit of $1.24 million, *All This and Heaven, Too* was Davis's biggest hit yet upon release in the winter of 1940, but her domestic chaos drained all joy from the distinction. At the Academy Awards ceremony in February 1940, Davis stalked from the hall the instant she lost the Best Actress trophy to Vivien Leigh – an impolite departure that she later attributed not to jealousy, but to complete exhaustion.

Only her second opportunity to work with William Wyler – in Davis's estimation, still far and away the best director in Hollywood – restored her good spirits. The pair teamed up again to make *The Letter*, another adaptation of a W Somerset Maugham short story, about a bored, dissolute Englishwoman living with her husband on a rubber plantation in Malaya. Maddened when her lover marries another woman, Davis's character Leslie Crosbie shoots him six times, then unflinchingly supplies the colonial police with an elaborate tale of attempted rape and self-defence. But though her descriptions of her ex-lover's assault never alter, Leslie's sang-froid gradually unravels with every interrogation. In this, her 43rd role in Hollywood, Davis drew on former mentor Martha Graham's lessons like never before, relying principally on hand gestures to convey Leslie's gradual loss of self-possession: the thicker her lies, the shakier her knitting; the cooler her pleas, the more clenched her palms. The result is what Kael called 'the best study of female sexual hypocrisy in history'.[106] It earned Davis yet another Oscar nomination.

Davis's second marriage to Arthur Farnsworth in 1940 took everyone by surprise, she would later describe him as the great love of her life.

Off-stage the grudges and tantrums continued. Wyler had married in the two years since his fling with Davis and wanted none of the by-then libertine actress's sexual advances. During *Jezebel*, Davis had obeyed her director's every suggestion, but the intervening years had made her far less tractable, and she surprised Wyler by challenging his interpretation of the climactic moment of the film; she went so far as to walk off the set in protest. Davis eventually bowed to Wyler's judgment, but the disagreement signalled the beginning of the end of their working relationship.

Davis returned to New Hampshire in the summer of 1940 to find the just-divorced Farnsworth determined to elevate his sometime romance with the movie queen into a more permanent venture. Though she had had many affairs since meeting Farnsworth the previous summer, Davis allowed him to escort her back to California, where she was slated to star in yet another drama of illegitimacy, *The Great Lie*. Davis caught the tabloid-writers off guard when she married her New Hampshire suitor at a friend's secluded Arizona ranch. Farnsworth was so little known in Hollywood at that time that even the omniscient gossip columnist Louella Parsons had to settle for describing him as 'a wealthy Boston businessman'.[107]

At the dawn of 1941, Davis had all she had ever wanted in life, both fame and love. That summer she saw her stature in Hollywood affirmed when she became the first woman ever elected president of the Academy of Motion Picture Arts and Sciences. Flattered and eager to take charge, the actress blazed into the first meeting armed with a thick agenda. She first proposed to prohibit extras from casting ballots in the Academy Award competition, pointing out that most never even watched the films they walked through. As fellow board members simply nodded, dismissing this and other fruits of her hard-won wisdom with blank smiles, Davis began to suspect that the Academy had selected her for her name, not her intelligence.

Too much the star to play figurehead, Davis resigned the position after only six weeks: another milestone in the history of the Academy. Darryl F Zanuck (1902–1979), the legendary studio head at Twentieth Century Fox, rang Davis to warn her that after spitting on such an accolade, she would 'never work in Hollywood again'.[108] Over the next few years, the mogul would come to regret his prediction, for during World War Two, Davis's power in Hollywood only grew.

Hollywood on the Home Front · 1940–1945

As the threat of another world war increased, Bette Davis entertained florid doubts about Hollywood's relevance to global events: *With France, beautiful brave France collapsing, England with its back to the wall, and Hitler's hordes trampling down democracy everywhere in Europe, making faces at motion-picture cameras seemed utterly inconsequential. My feeling about my work was, 'What does it matter?'*[110]

Davis's disparagement of Hollywood rings a false note, for as *Hitler's hordes* swept across the Continent, she was working harder than ever, behaving indeed as if nothing but Hollywood mattered. Granted, many actors in Hollywood (and Americans in general) took some years to register the threat of Hitler, but it is nevertheless striking that Davis never once mentions it in all her interviews in the 1930s.

The Great Depression first elevated Hollywood into the myth-maker of the nation, and World War Two did much to fortify the industry's cultural mission. The years 1941 to 1945 represented the zenith of the American film industry, both in terms of profit – in the revitalised wartime economy, studios sold an average of 90 million tickets every week – and of cultural influence. In the decade before TV invaded the American household, Hollywood served as the seismograph of popular sentiment and the barometer of public morality.

Almost immediately after America declared war in December of 1941, the great studios joined forces with the federal government to rally domestic support, producing military training films, morale-boosting pin-ups and star appearances for the soldiers. The industry's most important task was to stir pro-war sentiment at home. From Frank Capra's *Why We Fight* pictures (the most famous of which is *Know Your Enemy: Japan*) to Bugs Bunny's topical shorts at Warners (with equally telling titles like 'Herr meets Hare' and 'Bugs Bunny Nips the Nips'), no moviegoer could escape Hollywood's patriotic crusade. By 1945, even Westerns included a few evil Nazis for the righteous cowboy to shoot down.

Warner Brothers, at the insistence of Harry Warner, became the first studio to join the fight against Fascism. After the 1938 invasion of Austria, Harry closed Warners' German office. By 1939, when most of Hollywood was still tacitly accommodating Hitler, Warners tested public opinion with veiled parables of totalitarianism (*Juarez*, one of Davis's four blockbusters of 1939) and exposés of anti-Semitism (*The Life of Émile Zola*). The studio successfully dodged censure until it released the unambiguously anti-Hitler docudrama, *Confessions of a Nazi Spy*, enraging not just Hollywood's all-powerful censorship office but isolationists, Nazi sympathisers and citizens with German business interests.

Harry Warner, who managed Warner Brothers' finances from New York, had tracked Hitler's activities with keen interest since 1934. A far more observant Jew than his younger brother Jack, Harry was determined to use his studio's pictures to alert Americans to the threat abroad. He was in the minority in Hollywood, for even as the nationwide debate between isolationists and interventionists spread across the prairie, the movie industry remained strangely silent on the war question. It was, then, at considerable risk to the studio that Harry Warner vetoed Jack's profit-minded objections and took such an early stand against Nazism.

It was only the Japanese bombing of Pearl Harbor that legitimised the studio's audacity. As America prepared for war, Warners zoomed to the fore of Hollywood's pro-American campaign producing not just vigorously pro-war features like *Sergeant York* (1941) and *Pride of the Marines* (1945), but commercial-length public-service announcements. With a severe hairdo and kindly expression, Davis appeared in one of these film shorts. Flanked by two all-American children, Billy and Ginny, the actress gently explained why there would be no baseball bat or bike under the tree that Christmas: Mommy would be giving all their spare money to the Red Cross that year, in order to help Daddy, who was off 'fighting somewhere far, far away.'[111]

Some of Davis's personal contributions were just as theatrical; for example, when the government announced the rationing of all petrol, Davis jaunted around Los Angeles for a few days in a horse and carriage. Davis issued a wartime 'code' for American girls: *It should be our duties as American wives, sweethearts and mothers,* she said in an official government statement, *to unite to avoid any lowering of American morals. The length of skirts or the color of lipstick may be of great importance to some, but these difficult times should put an end to such foolishness.*[112]

Still a passionate liberal and FDR-admirer, Warners's top-grossing actress participated in the 'Stars Across America' programme in mid-1942, travelling to Missouri and Oklahoma to rally factory workers to purchase war bonds. Her rabble-rousing rhetoric, though blunt (*Do what you can do,* or *you're not my idea of an American!* she exhorted in one speech), proved extremely profitable.[113] She sold a record-breaking $2 million of bonds in just two days, a *Jezebel* portrait for $250,000, and a single autograph for $50,000. But though she delighted in these triumphs, her temper was already souring, and she demanded full salary for this fortnight of full-time patriotism. Jack Warner sternly refused any such compensation, lecturing Davis on her duties as an American. When Davis proceeded to point out the ever-increasing profits of her then 38 films for the studio, Warner compromised, raising her salary to $5,000 a week while restricting her output to three pictures a year.

In autumn of 1942, Davis became co-founder and President of the Hollywood Canteen, a star-run banquet hall for soldiers en route to the Pacific Theatre. From October 1942 to August 1945, the Canteen entertained 3,000 departing soldiers every night. Alongside fellow celebrities like Bing Crosby, Marlene Dietrich, Abbott and Costello, Duke Ellington, Rita Hayworth, Olivia de Havilland and Joan Crawford, Davis scrubbed floors and ladled soup. Under Davis, the Canteen was extraordinarily successful throughout the war; even after costing $3,000 a week to run, it closed in August 1945 with a surplus of half a million dollars.

To some degree, Davis even put aside her diva complex for Uncle Sam. In 1943, persuaded that her name would attract larger audiences to the anti-Fascist picture, she accepted a secondary role in Lillian Hellman's *Watch on the Rhine*. That same year, Davis, though accustomed to top billing, made an even smaller cameo in the musical *Thank Your Lucky Stars*, and along with other stars donated her $50,000 fee to the Canteen. In her enthusiasm for this fund-raising jamboree, Davis shed her self-seriousness and belted out 'They're Either too Young or Too Old' while jitterbugging with a GI. In 1944, Davis made her final onscreen contribution to the war in the charity picture, *The*

Davis raising funds and wartime morale in *The Hollywood Canteen* 1944

Hollywood Canteen, another performance distinguished by an uncommon display of levity.

I'm very proud of those war years, Davis said four decades later. *The boys never had any money, and they wanted to see movie stars. For some of them it was their last leave before going overseas. They all knew they might be killed the next week.*[114]

But among all her misty reminiscences – *the look in those service-men's eyes was all the reward I needed* – Davis neglected to mention the limits of her altruism.[115] In 1943, after her lover *du jour*, the director Vincent Sherman, stood her up on holiday in Acapulco, Davis furiously rejected Jack Warner's request that she grace the ribbon-cutting ceremony of the Mexican Red Cross. Sick, she said, of working *for free* even on her infrequent holidays, she demanded a high fee for this goodwill gesture, even after Warner reminded her of all the actors serving as unofficial ambassadors in Latin American countries to help the United States forge loyalties in the southern hemisphere.[116] When patriotism failed, Warner tried blatant narcissism, imploring Davis to take advantage of this 'wonderful opportunity . . . to be the great lady all Mexico knows you are'.[117]

Swayed by this irresistible logic, Davis succumbed to the burden of renown. During World War Two, she knew that it was not simply Mexico that recognised her as a 'great lady'. It was the entire world.

THE WOMEN'S PICTURE

Since the beginning of her career, Bette Davis had repeatedly bucked studio protocol by giving unusually candid interviews in the press. 'She's not your ordinary blue-eyed blonde, this Davis girl,' one of the earliest profiles began. 'She's ambitious, coura-geous, un-complaining[,] with a distinct mind of her own[,] will-ing to work for what she gets out of life; the world is too full of women – and men – who think it owes them a living.'[118] Later fea-tures confirmed this portrayal of a no-nonsense New Englander: 'Davis dislikes equally the stuffed shirts and glamour girls of Hollywood and makes no effort to please them . . . Informality is her keynote – she no longer dyes her hair and she never diets.'[119]

In public appearances Davis dished out eyebrow-raising remarks like *domesticity's all right if it isn't carried too far* and *a bitch*

The unrivalled queen of the 'women's picture' turned in another blockbusting and emotionally overwrought role in *Now, Voyager* 1942

is more memorable than a sweet housewife.[120] Warners' PR hounds initially feared the box-office consequences of Davis's unheard-of indelicacy, but over time the actress's outspokenness worked in her favour, winning her a formidable following composed almost exclusively of women. Davis's frequent indiscretions projected an image 'real' women could understand. Her well-publicised personal struggles – her failed romances, her job frustrations, her occasional abrasiveness – endeared her to fans experiencing similar life-management problems on a more modest scale.

Self-made, unafraid and fallible, Bette Davis came to embody the American dream of the girl next door becoming a star. For female audiences, it mattered that Davis owed her fame not to celestial beauty but to diligence, daring and honesty. Having played a succession of screen characters who succeed on the basis of persistence, cleverness and sometimes even connivance, Davis gave 'normal' women hope that, no matter what they looked like, they too could take charge of their fates, find love and attract husbands – perhaps even become movie stars. This message appealed to audiences that the celebrated critic and novelist James Agee derided as 'made up mainly of unloved and not easily lovable women'.[121] Agee later summed up Davis's cinematic speciality as a 'typical woman's duet on the standard musical saws favoured by any housewives' magazine (the tune is "Love is the Sweetest thing but we have no Bananas today")'.[122]

No film more explicitly illustrates women's identification with Davis than *Now, Voyager*, the chronicle of Charlotte Vale's spiritual, sexual and physical transformation. An inhibited old maid from a rich Boston family, Charlotte is on the verge of a nervous

'Oh Jerry, don't let's ask for the moon-we have the stars' The most gloriously schmaltzy line of Davis's whole career is from *Now, Voyager*

breakdown when her psychoanalyst advises her to escape her controlling mother and take a cruise to South America (originally Europe, but war necessitated a last-minute re-routing). There, dowdy 'Aunt Charlotte' meets Jerry, a sensitive man trapped in a marriage as loveless and oppressive as the Back Bay mansion where Charlotte grew up. The two outcasts fall in love and *voilà*: Davis drops the pillows bulking up her figure and strolls back on to the cabin deck streamlined and radiant, alive. But because love has exposed not only Charlotte's cheekbones but her morality, she refuses to consummate her passion for Jerry in the most gloriously schmaltzy line of Davis's entire screen career: *'Oh, Jerry, don't let's ask for the moon – we have the stars.'*

Now, Voyager was a huge hit upon its release in January 1942, less than a month after the invasion of Pearl Harbor. In this picture, which Pauline Kael described as a 'schlock classic', Charlotte's metamorphosis answered the prayers of millions of American women who had been raised to believe that redemption resided in the love of a good man – if only they could find one.[123] This message held a particular power that winter, and *Now, Voyager* netted the biggest profit of any Bette Davis film to date, and brought the actress her fifth consecutive Oscar nomination.

No less importantly, *Now, Voyager* cemented Davis's lead role in the reinvention of the 'women's picture'. Female-heavy features had steadily gained popularity throughout the 1930s (consider *Dark Victory*'s unexpected splash), but the outbreak of World War Two created a tremendous new demand for strong female examples on the screen. *We women had full sway for about ten years*, Davis once said, *from the mid-30s to mid-40s.*[124] As the draft drained the country of its movie-going men, war widows, anxious wives, spinsters and adolescent girls, all driven into intimidating positions of autonomy, sought instruction and consolation from headstrong women like the eponymous heroines of *Stella Dallas* (played by

Barbara Stanwyck), *Mildred Pierce* (Joan Crawford) and *Gilda* (Rita Hayworth). But none of these actresses proved so willing or natural a role model as Bette Davis.

However propitious in the early 1940s, Davis's woman-of-independent-means shtick was no mere marketing ploy. For as long as she had received top billing – and even before then, as Leslie Howard's experience in *Of Human Bondage* suggests – Davis tended to overwhelm the men who co-starred in her pictures, even ones as powerful as Errol Flynn and Paul Muni. Over the course of her decade-long career in Hollywood, she had played her fair share of gangsters' molls and submissive girlfriends, but in the roles that made Davis famous, the men seldom had a chance to steal the show: witness Henry Fonda's fine, but ultimately forgotten, performance in *Jezebel*, or George Brent's sensitive anonymity in *Dark Victory.*

But just as *domesticity's all right if it isn't carried too far*, independence is all right if it doesn't imperil attractiveness. The more this harpy persona defined her onscreen, the more Davis attempted to soften it in the fan magazines. *The Great Fuss is in vain*, she told *Photoplay* magazine. *Women never have, never will, never can be independent of the men they love – and be happy! All women know this . . . Men should boss women more! Women adore feeling they are possessed, and they belong to a dominant male.*[125]

In reality, however, as in her films, Davis had trouble sharing the stage with her male escort. Although she purported to pine for a strong man – a decision-maker, leader and protector – she had never displayed any great aptitude for subjugation. Her father's abandonment had very early on established feelings of discomfort – both insecurity and contempt – with the opposite sex, and since her trials as a neophyte stage actress, Davis had fought with men. In her prime, she was notorious with directors as much for terrorising as for seducing them. Alpha males – most notably Jack Warner – had never much admired Davis's strong side, and

No actor ever stole the show from Bette Davis. Going through her lines with Paul Heinreid on the set of *Now, Voyager* 1942

the actress often wondered w*hat was it about me that created resistance in these men.*[126]

Instead, Davis gravitated to the weaker-willed in her choice of both lovers and directors, men who submitted to her authority and never second-guessed her whims. Had she not handpicked her playboy second husband for his lack of a distinct job or discernible spine? But where Davis could rule, she could never respect. If there was any truth in her claims that she was *divinely happy* with Farnsworth, it owed much to the couple's long-distance relationship, which continued after they were married.[127] Within a month of their December 1940 wedding, Farnsworth took an improbable job defrosting aeroplane wings in Minneapolis. His full-time commuting suited Davis's workaholic schedule beautifully; it also allowed her to continue cheating on him at every opportunity.

Years later, Davis admitted that she had swiftly seen her dashing New Englishman for what he really was: *an alcoholic who was tied to his mother's apron strings*.[128] In the summer of 1943, after her abortive rendezvous in Acapulco with director Vincent Sherman, Davis stormed back to New Hampshire in a final bid to resuscitate her marriage. But by that late stage no play-acted rusticity could blind her to her second husband's alcoholism, laziness and general boorishness, and she soon returned to California, hoping to cushion her unhappiness in a flurry of thespian activity. But no sooner had Farnsworth followed her back to California than, on the afternoon of 23 August 1943, he fell head first on to the pavement, fracturing his skull. He died the next evening without having regained consciousness. The coroner identified the cause of death not as the accident on Hollywood Boulevard, but as a blood clot resulting from a fracture inflicted about a fortnight earlier. Asked about the possible circumstances of this previous injury at the inquest, Farnsworth's high-profile widow remembered an incident in New Hampshire that June when her husband had tripped while rushing to answer the phone – an unsatisfactory explanation, since Davis had placed the incident two months, not weeks, before her husband's death. The coroner never resolved this mystery, for that same week the omnipotent Jack Warner, anxious lest unseemly rumours tarnish his top commodity's reputation, hastily secured an 'accidental death' verdict to shelve all future enquiries. The inquest ended up reporting the exact opposite of the autopsy, but Warner's sway was such that the questions ceased immediately.

A horse-riding accident, a motel room scuffle with a cuckolded husband, a blow from the butt of a gun – gossip about the cause of death of the great star's husband continued to circulate, in spite of the coroner's verdict. Most of it was generated by Bette Davis herself. Already bored by widowhood in late 1943, the actress began advancing many contradictory hypotheses about her husband's mysterious collapse, telling anyone who would listen that Farnsworth's briefcase had vanished from the scene of the accident. Several weeks afterwards, Davis claimed, a Dickensian urchin had crept into her dressing room one day, bearing Farnsworth's briefcase and confessing that he had snatched it in the hubbub on Hollywood Boulevard. The boy then compounded the bereaved widow's shock by revealing the contents of the briefcase – half a dozen empty bottles of booze – thereby confirming Davis's suspicions about how husband number two passed his days without her. Later, Davis even hinted that Farnsworth's bizarre wing-defrosting work in Minnesota had served as a cover for top-secret war work, and that he had been assassinated for the contents of his briefcase.

As the years wore on, Davis – who in her 1961 autobiography admitted that *I was not violently in love with Farney. I loved his loving me and our mutual love of the New England way of life was the tie that finally bound* – grew fonder of Farnsworth in hindsight; at least he had performed the service of expiring dramatically.[129] Toward the end of her own life, the lonely ex-legend took to eulogising Farnsworth as the great love of her life – the 'One' whom Cruel Fate had robbed her of.

With Farnsworth gone, Davis abandoned herself to high-impact mourning in the form of back-alley affairs with Hollywood Canteen's enlisted customers. Almost every evening at the Canteen, Davis would steal off with another soldier, hoping every time to stumble upon the love she had never quite achieved with her first two husbands.

To judge by her romantic entanglements, Bette Davis was less liberated than lonely, and suffered problems similar to those of her self-reliant heroines onscreen. *I always knew that I would end up alone,* she said toward the end of her life, commenting on the title of her 1961 autobiography, *The Lonely Life*.[130] Even if she had unwittingly invited her independence, she by no means welcomed it.

THE HORRORS OF EGOCENTRICITY
ON A MARATHONIC SCALE

In the early 1930s, as the cultural dominion of Hollywood began to alarm the more conservative sectors of American society, a puritanical Production Code came into existence in Hollywood, established to protect unsuspecting citizens from the moral taint of the movies. As promulgated by the reactionary Joseph Breen, the Production Code banned, among other things, expletives, toilets, shared beds and tight sweaters. The Code had existed since 1921, when the film industry first imposed censorship on itself by establishing the Motion Picture Producers and Distributors of America (MPPDA), an organisation that would become synonymous with the Motion Picture Production Code. After Catholic bishops formed the Legion of Decency in 1934 to prevent American morals from being polluted in the cinema, the Production Code took an even greater role in controlling the content of Hollywood movies. Breen went to great lengths to enforce the Code's understanding of natural justice, which explains why, in classic Hollywood cinema, if characters are sometimes permitted to sin, they cannot escape punishment for their wrongdoings.

This Old Testament stricture influenced the outcomes of many Bette Davis movies, particularly those featuring the hell-bent bitches she loved to play best. Take the sombre lessons of *Jezebel*: Julie Marsden can defy society all she likes, but she cannot expect ever to be admitted into it again. Though Julie decides to wear the scandalous red dress to the ball more out of idleness and arrogance than conviction, the ill-considered act costs her not only her place in New Orleans society, but also her fiancé. The original denouement of Somerset Maugham's *The Letter* hinges on the ambiguous moral implications of Leslie Crosbie's acquittal. But Hollywood had no patience for ambiguity or implication. Breen demanded that Maugham's salacious story be revised so that Davis's character die for her transgressions.

On countless occasions in her films, Davis's characters had to learn that ruin is not reversible and that repentance, should it come too late, carries no promise of redemption. In life, however, the actress was slower to absorb this warning. By the time she was 35 – the *best age for a woman*, she declared, for *you don't make a fool of yourself as much as you did when younger, and you're old enough to call the shots* – she was one of the most important stars in the business.[131] But her taste for power had grown in direct proportion to her box-office returns: as her fame became legendary, so did her sense of entitlement. One of the actress's most frequently cited theatre adages – *The worse the rehearsals, the better the finished product* – applied to so many of her wartime hits that she came to delight in the problems marring her productions: the tantrums, the accusations and the sackings. *Once I had box-office clout,* Davis said, *I never let Warner forget it* – or, for that matter, any other colleague.[132]

The behind-the-scenes fighting that had characterised the making of her 1939 hits, *The Old Maid* and *The Private Lives of Elizabeth and Essex*, escalated alarmingly in the 1940s. With every success, Davis exercised less restraint on the soundstage. Those who worked under her – that is to say, nearly everyone – had no choice but to tolerate her erratic behaviour. Still, some of her new enemies, in particular William Wyler, the director Davis respected above all others, had more leverage.

Even though the two control-freaks had already clashed while filming *The Letter* the previous year, their professional relationship was still sufficiently cordial for Davis to agree to spend one of her rare holidays making *The Little Foxes* with Wyler at his studio, Samuel Goldwyn. But star and director began to disagree over

In the role of Regina Giddens in Hollywood's *The Little Foxes* Davis updated the role that Tallulah Bankhead had made famous on Broadway, there was no love lost between the actresses

their interpretations of Davis's character, Regina Giddens, almost immediately. Like the playwright of *The Little Foxes*, Lillian Hellman, Wyler imagined the celluloid Regina exactly as Tallulah Bankhead had portrayed her in the popular stage version – at once charismatic and manipulative, seductive and deadly. Davis, however, had other ideas. Without consulting her director, she decided that her Regina would be brittle and cold, shorn of sensuality.

Wyler found Davis's determination to differentiate herself from Bankhead extremely odd, for the actress had inherited several of her best-loved roles from stage actresses with no discernible anxiety of influence, including Lynn Fontane's Queen in *Elizabeth and Essex*, Katharine Cornell's adulteress in *The Letter* and Miriam Hopkins's brat in *Jezebel*. She was both known and celebrated for her ability to update these stage characterisations for the screen. Indeed, only two years before *The Little Foxes*, Davis had come very close to copying Bankhead's Judith Traherne in *Dark Victory*. Wyler early on suspected that his leading lady's resistance owed more to obstinacy than art. Perhaps her spurned romantic overtures during *The Letter* were informing her current attitude. 'Boy, did it irritate me to read that I was making her copy Tallulah!' Wyler fumed in an interview. 'That wasn't true. I was just making her play Regina Giddens and not Bette Davis.'[133]

Wyler makes a serious charge: that narcissism had blunted Davis's sensitivity to character and, more broadly, eroded her skills as an actress. His observation would prove remarkably prescient in the years to come, as Bette Davis, no longer toasted for self-reliance, came to be ridiculed for self-caricature. In 1941, however,

Tallulah Bankhead (1903–1968), the daughter of a prominent Alabama political family and the pre-eminent stage actress of her generation, was one of the century's most flamboyant and controversial personalities. Famously bisexual and still celebrated (particularly by drag queens) for her throaty voice and signature 'Dahhling', Bankhead possessed a tremendous, if often ungenerous, wit. 'The less I behave like Whistler's mother the night before, the more I look like her the morning after', she once quipped.[134] Though her dominion over Broadway was unchallenged, Bankhead got only a toehold in Hollywood, and every failure fanned her hatred of Bette Davis. 'When I get hold of Bette Davis,' she once said, 'I'm going to tear every hair out of her . . ,. moustache!'[135] In the 1950s, incensed by what she considered the scandalous similarities between her and Davis's character in *All About Eve*, Bankhead broadcast her resentments on her radio show. Davis offers only this suspiciously mild account of her one meeting with Bankhead: *I was standing at the bar when up swept Tallulah,* she recalled. *I was a bit anxious about what her behaviour would be. 'Dahling,' she said, 'You've played all the parts I've played, and I was so much better.' 'I agree with you, Miss Bankhead,' I said. She wafted quickly out of the room. She didn't get the fight she wanted.*[136]

she was still the Queen of Hollywood and in *The Little Foxes* not even William Wyler could stop her from screeching instead of speaking and gyrating instead of gesturing. Whenever Wyler objected to the clownish Constitutional Convention wig she insisted on donning, Davis would douse her ornamental hairpiece with more Kabuki powder; whenever he attempted to moderate the fusillade-pace of her line delivery, Davis would only pull her lips all the tighter and raise her voice all the louder.

Their disputes soon grew so venomous that Davis threatened to walk off the picture. Wyler had to capitulate completely to lure her back, but he was not a man to surrender lightly. Although Davis saw her controversial interpretation of Regina Giddens validated by yet another Oscar nomination, this institutional honour ill compensated for her destruction of Wyler's respect. It is true that the spectacular closing scene of *The Little Foxes* – in which Davis watches Herbert Marshall, who plays her husband, crawling across the floor for his heart medicine – relied on her harsher characterisation of Regina Giddens, but Wyler never came around to this point of view. For the rest of her life, the actress pined for the chance to make *one more film with Willie before I end my career*, Wyler, for his part, did his utmost to ensure that no such misfortune ever befell him again.[137]

Wyler's criticism about the actress's tendency to 'play Bette Davis' applied equally to her next big vehicle, the plantation drama *In This Our Life* (1942). Many reviewers remarked on similarities between Regina Giddens and Davis's latest virago, Stanley Timberlake. Over the course of stealing her sister's husband, knocking down an innocent child while driving her convertible, and finally blaming the hit-and-run on a servant, Davis, whose eyeballs threaten to pop right into the stalls, is almost indistinguishable from her previous incarnation. In both films the histrionic excess is affecting but whether as opera, vaudeville or science fiction it is difficult to establish. 'There is something elemental about Bette,' said John Huston, director of *In This Our Life*, 'a demon within her which threatens to break out and eat everybody, beginning with their ears.'[138] The ad campaign for the movie played up the popularity of Davis's evil roles with the slogan, *No one's as good as Bette when she's bad!*

Was the problem that on paper Regina and Stanley share several salient characteristics – both are scheming Confederate villainesses with cash – or that Davis had lost the ability to interpret subtle differences between roles? Typecasting certainly hindered Davis less than her increasing tendency to let personal grudges distort her performances. Though she had no great axe to grind with John Huston, Davis made no secret of resenting his declared passion for her co-star, Olivia de Havilland. She acted up accordingly, engaging in elaborate time-wasting attention-getting devices designed to remind Huston who the *real* star of the picture was.

Despite these difficulties – by then standard on a Bette Davis production – World War Two audiences ate up *In This Our Life*, a chronicle of a strong-willed female taking charge of her life that still stands as another great example of the 'women's picture'. Of course, as both Regina Giddens and Stanley Timberlake learn the hard way, strength need not equal virtue, and independence often has little bearing on goodness. Unlike Charlotte Vale in Davis's subsequent film, *Now, Voyager* – a character who finds peace in solitude and elevates renunciation into redemption – Regina and Stanley never make good on their self-sufficiency. One is forsaken, the other killed for her sins, and the advantages that both fought so long to obtain shrivel up unused. The comparison is obvious but unavoidable: like Regina and Stanley, Bette Davis was developing the unfortunate habit of wielding her power gratuitously, laying waste to its real rewards.

And yet not all punishments are instantaneous, and as long as her gyrations turned high profits, Jack Warner would give the star *carte blanche* to flail and hiss and play Bette Davis as much as she liked. After the reception of *In This Our Life*, Warner even accepted Davis's recommendation of Irving Rapper to direct *Now, Voyager* – chosen not because she respected the relatively inexperienced newcomer, but because she judged him insecure and easily dominated. After heavy-hitters like Wyler and Huston, she needed the break. It seems, then, paradoxical that Davis, in her interpretation of Charlotte Vale, avoided the maenadic furore of Regina Giddens and Stanley Timberlake, for in life the actress intended no such retreat.

From the outset Davis ruled the roost, rewriting the script, ordering around the cast and subjugating the crew. 'She would take on Irving in front of everybody,'[139] one underling remembered. 'She had to control everything and everybody.' Davis, in response to these charges, merely said that she felt *rudderless* under Rapper.[140]

Three years later, when they worked together again on *The Corn Is Green*, Davis took even more extreme measures to flout Rapper's authority, from donning an inappropriately oversized wig for her role as a 60-something schoolmistress to volcanically overreacting when the flap of a broken lighting fixture grazed her head. Soon fed up with these 'eccentricities', Rapper charged Davis with ruining the film with her 'tantrums' and 'sadistic bullying'.[141] A member of the crew recalls Davis's fiery reply: *Tantrums! Sadistic! Listen, you no-talent third-rater, you ought to go down on your knobby knees in gratitude that you're directing a Bette Davis picture!*[142] It was Rapper who reportedly roared of Davis, 'What she needs is a psychiatrist, not a director!'[143]

By 1945, Davis's outbursts had long since removed her from the list of serious Oscar contenders – *The Corn Is Green* would end her six-year streak of Best Actress nominations – but in January 1942, when *Now, Voyager* hit the screens, Davis seemed invincible. Like never before, *Now, Voyager*'s triumph authorised her meddling and seemed to prove that the true star needs no director. Davis showed her fangs so early on in the making of her next film, *Old Acquaintance*, in which she was paired opposite her one-time nemesis Miriam Hopkins, that the director feigned a heart attack to escape the assignment. *In those years I made many enemies*, Davis said much later. *When I was most unhappy I lashed out rather than whined.*[144]

Davis always insisted, however, that reports of her misbehaviour were grossly exaggerated. *Do I act like a monster?* she appealed to one interviewer. *No, it wasn't justified . . . It was part of the Bette Davis legend . . . It became very fashionable to say that you had directed me and survived.*[145] She also denied any mean-spirited motivation for the havoc she seemed almost automatically to unleash: *I fought battles for little people who weren't in a position to stand up for themselves*, she said. *I got a reputation for being difficult – a reputation that still plagues me today. But I wasn't and I'm not. All I ever wanted – or want now – is professionalism.*

Professionalism was a familiar defence from Davis, one that became less credible with every project. *Mr Skeffington* in 1944, no less than *Of Human Bondage* and *Jezebel*, marked a turning point in Davis's career. But while those earlier milestones marked refinements in her craft, *Skeffington* had quite the opposite significance: it was the first time that Davis's misconduct not only delayed, but came very close to destroying, a film with her name above the title. To be fair to Davis, production began the week before Farnsworth's death. Although Warner himself had recommended that Davis take a leave of absence, the actress – a great believer in the healing powers of Hollywood – reported on the set after only a few days of cursory mourning.

Davis's resilience doubtless owed something to her impatience to play – for the first time in her career, and in glorious contravention of everything expected of the Little Brown Wren – a deadly beauty and remorseless femme fatale. Apparently the thrill of Fanny Trellis's characterisation faded fast, Davis went to heroic lengths to upset the production schedule. Not only did she refuse to play the scenes as written, she added so many absurd flourishes that the first cut of the film ran 3 hours and 20 minutes. She bulldozed all advice, whether it pertained to lines, call times or cosmetics. For the final scenes of *Mr Skeffington*, after diphtheria has ravaged Fanny's famously lovely complexion, Davis – who had long prided herself on using make-up to enhance the authenticity of her roles – slathered on opaque rubbery clown make-up, with results that were far more drag queen than fallen angel. When the director, Vincent Sherman, implored Davis to moderate her grotesqueness, Davis dismissed him with a telling comment. *Don't worry about it,* she shrugged, *my fans love me to do something like this.*[146]

One afternoon, while working on *Mr Skeffington*, Davis mistook ammonia for eyewash and scalded herself with the solution. Afterwards she skittered hysterically around the soundstage, parading her paranoia and psychosis by accusing everyone in sight of conspiring to murder her. Acknowledging that Davis's unpopularity gave some weight to her accusations, the film's producer quipped that the police 'could have rounded up any number of likely perpetrators'.

'There isn't a damn thing that can be done as long as Bette Davis is the director,' the unit manager grumbled as the shooting fell two months behind schedule.[147] As the actress showed no sign of improving, the film's desperate producers entertained the scandalous possibility of cutting their losses and abandoning the project. When the panicked director detailed the 'Bette Davis problem' to his wife, she guardedly consented to his conducting a brief affair with his leading lady. Davis's behaviour altered overnight, and within a week the young widow was browbeating Sherman to leave his wife for her. The director, however, had already made up his mind that ' no matter what happened I could never marry a woman like this,' and the same week that he wrapped the film, split with Davis.[148]

Mr Skeffington eventually opened to respectable notices and profits, and Davis even received her sixth consecutive Best Actress nomination for the film, but few believed that she had earned it. James Agee anticipated the public's inevitable boredom with watching Bette Davis play herself in a single phrase, dismissing *Mr Skeffington* as 'just another of those pictures in which Bette Davis demonstrates the horrors of egocentricity on a marathonic scale'.[149] In short, although fame brought Bette Davis respect, sycophancy, even sex, it also destroyed the last shreds of humility in an ego that was dangerously outsized from the start. As per the moral law of Hollywood, all horrors must come home to roost.

Back then, critics and fans applauded Davis's daring. But they were soon to discover that the line between art and kitsch is very fine indeed. Davis's skilful mannerisms, once the linchpin of her histrionic brilliance, required great measures of self-control. Without restraint, Davis's flailing style and intentionally wild appearance – as her audience, if not the actress herself, would learn over the years ahead – eroded into self-parody.

As her aggressively silly performance in *Mr Skeffington* showed, Davis was beginning to rely on her grotesqueries less to supplement than to replace the subtler aspects of her performances. The most famous film of Davis's later years, *Whatever Happened to Baby Jane?* (1962), provides grim evidence of what happens to an actress who wages a one-upmanship campaign against herself. After 30 years of shock-value makeovers, Davis slopped on so much pancake make-up and fire-hydrant lipstick that Baby Jane resembled less a semi-deranged ex-child-star than a hired clown at a child's birthday party. Between shivers, it is hard, at times, not to laugh. *Sometimes I even outdid myself, and it hurt*, Davis admitted. *When I first saw myself as Baby Jane, I cried.*[150]

The Last Chance • 1946–1960

When she arrived in Hollywood in December of 1930, Bette Davis still clung to her stage-training snobbery. She professed unmitigated scorn for the motion picture industry, proclaiming at every opportunity that *I was not fooled for a moment into thinking that the screen was the same thing as the stage.*[151] But once Davis, absolute in all her convictions, had submitted to *the miraculous power of the motion picture*, she never looked back.[152] By the mid-1930s, she was criticising colleagues for pretensions remarkably similar to those that she had only recently espoused. Of her occasional co-star Leslie Howard, for example, she scoffed: *Leslie was very snobbish about film. He let everyone know he was a stage actor, and only made pictures for money. It has always annoyed me that some Broadway stars treat Hollywood with contempt – as if they're slumming.*[153]

Twenty years later, Davis would channel this venom toward television, which she blamed for the demise of the sacred studio system and, by extension, her career. *People that have been bred on television production have no sense of pacing or style*, she snarled in 1976, characteristically forgetting that it was that same trashy medium that had kept her fed over the preceding two decades.[154]

With the war over and Americans relocating *en masse* to the suburbs, the reliable urban population of movie-goers shrank. Television overtook cinema as the predominant form of popular entertainment. After an all-time peak in ticket sales in 1946, movie attendance dropped steadily between 1947 and 1963, forcing all the major studios to use any means possible to stay afloat, even if that necessitated buying into the corrupt new medium.

(Ironically, though Jack Warner more than shared Davis's contempt for television, it was eventually the 'Merrie Melodies' cartoons, broadcast in American households every Saturday morning, that rescued his studio from bankruptcy.)

In 1938, well before the small screen began its onslaught, the moguls had already faced a serious threat when the federal government charged the major studios with illegal restraint of trade, the same kind of monopolistic practice that had undone the Edison Trust a quarter-century earlier. The Justice Department had to wait out the war, for a decision so that it was only in 1948 that the Supreme Court ruled the studio system's vertical monopoly unconstitutional and ordered the studios to divest themselves of their first-run theatres. The decision, known as the Paramount Decree, expedited the deterioration of the Big Five's assembly-line production system and – by opening the doors to European filmmakers and independent domestic producers – effectively ended the heyday of the mogul. In February 1949, after two of the majors – RKO and Paramount – had already bowed to the Decree, Harry Warner vowed not to give up their cinemas without a court fight. But for all this chest-thumping, Warner was only staying his own execution. By the 1960s, the major studios had so few assets left that multi-national corporations absorbed them as tax write-offs.

As if contending with these infrastructural changes weren't enough, Bette Davis had other murky challenges to face after the war. No less violently than in 1927, when the birth of talkies extinguished silent films overnight, the end of World War Two killed off the 'women's picture' that Davis had pioneered in films like *Dark Victory* and *Now, Voyager*. As a nation of husbands, back from the war, began clamouring for fresh-cooked dinners once again, the devoted wife contingent of Davis's fan-base could no longer enjoy the luxury of going to the movies two or three times a week. *During the war, women had done men's jobs*, Davis said, but afterwards, *Hollywood must have thought that the best way to get women back in their traditional place was by going back a few decades on the screen. Careers were out, home was in.*[155]

In the reactionary climate of post-war America, as female-heavy tearjerkers ceded to fast-paced combat pictures of a distinctly masculine odour, Davis's Hear Me Roar routine met with few sympathisers. *Women loved me,* Davis had never been loath to concede, *but many of their husbands hated me and stayed at home! I didn't play the 'little woman'.*[156] Unluckily for her, the *'little woman'* had come back into fashion: the only females men could tolerate watching onscreen were pining wives and doting mothers. By 1950, in fact, the election of Eisenhower saw these values reflected in the emergence of a new generation of soft-spoken actresses – Marilyn Monroe, Lana Turner, Doris Day – whom Davis scorned in aggregate as *the passive blonde.*[157]

Many of Davis's most illustrious contemporaries, including Marlene Dietrich, Greer Garson, Joan Crawford and Rosalind Russell, managed to adapt their images to this sterner era. To save their careers, the fast-talking newspaper girls of the 1930s metamorphosed into humourless matrons, the proud spinsters into grieving widows. Only Bette Davis, never a creature of great malleability, struggled in vain. She had, it seemed, too long been successful in the same thunder-and-lightning roles to shift back to the more reserved characters of her early years in Hollywood. Once again, it was James Agee, writing after the March 1945 release of *The Corn Is Green*, who put his finger on the actress's particular problem: 'I like and respect Miss Davis as a most unusually sincere and hardworking actress, and I have seen her play extremely well, but I did not find much in this performance to bring one beyond liking, respect, and, I am afraid, a kind of sympathy which no healthily functioning artist needs. It seems to me she is quite limited, which may be no sin but it is a pity, and that she is limiting herself beyond her rights by becoming more and more set, official and first-ladyish in mannerism and spirit, which is perhaps a sin as well as a pity.'[158]

Had these 'first-ladyish' mannerisms dulled her tastes as much as her performances? That seemed the case immediately after the war, when Jack Warner gave Davis the freedom to take charge of her image – not just in the magazines but in her movies as well – by agreeing to invest in an independent production company that permitted Davis to make five films of her own choosing. After almost 15 years of entreaties for *good scripts, good directors*, Davis could finally pick her own actors, cinematographers, even her own vehicles.[159] Ecstatic, she christened the company 'BD Inc' in glorious tribute to the personal power that she had, at such a cost, gained over her boss.

Jack Warner had not taken this step without reservations, but if the last few years had taught him to fear Davis's abuses of power, he hoped that new responsibilities might keep her demonic energies in check. He still couldn't help dreading Davis's highbrow pretensions – shuddering whenever the actress mentioned an adaptation of *Ethan Frome*, or a biography of Mary Todd Lincoln – so was greatly relieved (if also a little dumbfounded) when Davis announced that her first project with BD Inc would be a remake of *A Stolen Life*, a 1939 pot-boiler about twin sisters who fall for the same man. A far cry from the high art hogwash that Warner had come to expect from the actress, *A Stolen Life* seemed eminently palatable to the public taste, indeed almost a textbook example of Warners' own assembly-line output. Rather than vindicate her sophistication, *A Stolen Life* suggested that Davis no longer bothered herself much with high art, or Ibsen, or immortality, either because she had absorbed the studio's commercial priorities, or she had grown too complacent to care. In any event, the thrill of playing herself in duplicate – *It* is *balm for your ego*! – eclipsed any 'artistic' ambitions Davis might still have harboured; Mary Todd Lincoln just didn't have enough lines.[160]

What surprised Warner even more than Davis's silly script was the total lack of interest she demonstrated in all aspects of producing *A Stolen Life* – bizarre given the actress's notoriety for overhauling scripts and backseat directing in the past. In the winter of 1946, as pre-production got underway in the studios back in California, Davis was camped out near an army base in Georgia, too consumed with courting Corporal Lewis Riley, one of the strapping servicemen she had met at the Canteen, to oversee the details of her first independent production. Time and again she left unanswered the urgent telegrams Warner dispatched her. 'Despite what she claims in her autobiography she did *not* produce the picture,' the film's director, Curtis Bernhardt, complained. 'I'll face her any day on that. It had, in fact, no official producer. I was stuck with both ends of the thing, with producing and directing . . .'[161] *I simply meddled as usual*, Davis said, too breezy to disagree. *If that was producing, I had been a mogul for years*.[162] She only returned to California at the last possible moment, and once there she was no more cooperative than in the past: showing up late or not at all, throwing tantrums, interrupting takes – treating her own project like just another Warners' B-picture with her name above the title.

Released in May of 1946, *A Stolen Life* earned a record $2.5 million at the box office, but to most reviewers sitting through this 'distressingly empty piece of show-off', Davis's double role did little more than accentuate her immense – and offensive – self-regard.[163] Once again she received no mention in that year's Best Actress nominations, and in the end, Davis's flirtation with 'moguldom' confirmed what many detractors had long suspected – that she would rather throw fits than make decisions, rather hijack other people's power than exercise her own. The next winter, she dissolved BD Inc without ever attempting to make another picture.

Jack Warner welcomed Davis's retreat. Despite the box-office rewards of *A Stolen Life*, he, like many reviewers, was already detecting a pattern of decline in Davis's market value. In his cost-cutting efforts after the war, he had, in fact, already examined Davis's weekly salary of $6,000 to determine if she still earned it. The dismal reception of Davis's next film, *Deception*, clinched Warner's conviction that all actors have a shelf life, and only moguls rule forever. After an astonishing sequence of 49 straight hits, a film with the words 'Bette Davis' above the title had lost money. It

Bette busy losing the plot in the critical disaster *Beyond the Forest* 1948

had lost a great deal of money, too: half a million dollars. Though devastated, Davis saw the failure as an aberration; for Warner, it sounded the first alarm. As his contract player rounded the corner on her 40th birthday, Warner steeled himself for her downfall.

When Davis disbanded BD Inc in early 1947 and requested maternity leave, Warner consented with uncharacteristic alacrity, even volunteering to pay her for its duration. Fast bored by domesticity, Davis rushed back to California only three months after giving birth to her daughter in May of 1947. She longed for the perfect role to revitalise her career, but – having wound up BD Inc – she no longer had any say in what that role would be. Still, Davis appeared content when Warner offered her *Winter Meeting*, a 'prestige picture' about the unutterable love between a scholarly virgin and a war hero with a passion for the priesthood. Released in April of 1948, just two days after Davis turned 40, *Winter Meeting* lost almost a million dollars at the box office. Critics reviled it, and audiences simply ignored it. Blaming what

Newsweek generously called a 'thoroughly honest failure' on the Production Code's censorship of the thwarted sexual attraction between the bookish spinster and the spiritually inclined sailor, at no point did Davis acknowledge how irrevocably motherhood had aged her. Warning signs of fading beauty had certainly diminished her drawing power in *Deception*, but in *Winter Meeting* the once waif-like wren is puffy and fat, irremediably middle-aged – nothing even the saddest spinster cared to emulate.

Even after her next film, *June Bride*, failed to restore her status, Davis still possessed enough leverage at Warners to renegotiate a four-year contract in January 1949. Its lavish terms – $10,285 a week for only one picture a year, by far the largest salary she had ever received – betrayed none of Warner's qualms about keeping such an expensive actress on the payroll, but, unfortunately for Davis, the first picture she made under this contract, *Beyond the Forest*, was so scandalously bad that even her long-time defender the all-powerful celebrity columnist Hedda Hopper commented that 'if Bette had deliberately set out to wreck her career, she could not have picked a more appropriate vehicle.'[164]

Destined to become a key item in the Davis canon of camp, the highly entertaining *Beyond the Forest* is essential to understanding the undoing of Bette Davis as a performer. Granted, her self-control had been slipping for years, but here all remaining traces of restraint – all proportion, all plausibility – have disappeared, never again to return. The script of *Beyond the Forest* is a jumble of climaxes, spasms and overwrought exclamations to the tune of *What a dump!* (the line Elizabeth Taylor as Martha quotes in Edward Albee's *Who's Afraid of Virginia Woolf?* in 1962) and *If I don't get out of here, I'll die; If I don't get out of here, I hope I'll die*. As Rosa Moline, a dumpy, self-delusively 'sensual' housewife who demands more from life than the gentle, small-fry husband Fate has allotted her (described in the ad copy as 'a twelve o'clock girl in a nine o'clock town') Davis takes her taste for the overblown to the limit. No virgin, she, Davis tramps across the screen in roomy lumberjack shirts tied at the waist to showcase a most un-svelte abdomen (*the worst I'd ever looked on screen up to that time*, Davis admitted).[165] She purses her lips, smeared in clown-red lipstick, and poses seductively in canoes. She howls and shrieks and registers not a single credible emotion in the entire film.

I can't stand it here anymore! Rosa Moline explodes toward the film's spine-tingling denouement, an exclamation that well expressed Davis's frustrations with Warner Brothers. *I was so unhappy, and raised so much hell*, she said of her much-criticised misbehaviour during the making of the film.[166] As if excusing its consequences, Davis would later imply that she threatened to ditch the project mid-stream, consenting to finish it only if Jack Warner – who had already spent $800,000 on the picture – absolved her of all further obligations to the studio. To this day Hollywood historians argue about the abrupt termination of Davis's contract, which took place during a single 3 am phone call between her and Jack Warner. Whatever the precise chain of events, their disagreement, rooted in the actress's long-time discontent and Warner's growing belief that, at the age of 41, Bette Davis had 'lost her position as a sure money-maker for the studio', triggered her departure from the studio where she had worked for almost two decades.[167]

While the press cited Warners' unhappiness with Davis's box-office grosses as the reason for the split, the actress had quite a different spin: *After 18 years together*, her telegram to the press began, *this 'professional divorce' is the result of my long-standing wish to be relieved of any contractual obligations in order to have a wider choice of stories than is now possible at any one studio. I am most appreciative to Mr JL Warner for his consideration of my request.*[168]

Perhaps she had overstayed her welcome. In August of 1949, as she left Warner Brothers for the last time as a contract player, not a single colleague appeared at the gates to wish her well. Davis would later wax lyrical about her career at Warners, calling her time there the best 18 years of her life, but in August 1949, she only bid good riddance.

FROM DARKNESS TO *EVE*

Bette Davis had grown up surrounded by women left to fend for themselves in a world of men. In her first decade in Hollywood, the actress who called her father's influence negligible had clawed her way to the top of the most unabashedly male-orientated studio in Hollywood, in the process making the leap from chastity to promiscuity with remarkable ease. But even after countless high-profile affairs, her father's abandonment continued to set the tone of her romantic relationships, and she confronted lovers with a toxic mixture of dependency and distrust. Davis also remained desperately insecure about her appearance even at the apogee of her fame, and never tired of reminding interviewers that *I had the good fortune not to be a beautiful, beautiful raving beauty like Miss Hayworth, like Miss Everybody – Miss Harlow and all that.*[169]

After her first two marriages, to Ham Nelson and Arthur Farnsworth, both ended in long fade-outs, Davis became increasingly convinced that love and marriage represented no more than – in her own famous words – *a necessary refreshment, a comma, a dash in my life sentence of work.*[170] This conviction scarcely changed after she got married for the third time, to William Grant Sherry, on 27 November 1945.

In the year before this hasty south-of-the-border ceremony, Davis had dallied with many departing servicemen at the Hollywood Canteen, but until she met Corporal Lewis Riley, a wealthy New York businessman 12 years her junior, no tryst had rivalled the distractions of a good motion picture. When Riley was transferred to a training base in Georgia at the end of 1944, Davis dragged her sister across the country and set up camp across from his base. The sisters spent several peaceful months there. As the elder sister focused on extracting a marriage proposal, Bobby, who was still recovering from the painful disintegration of her own second marriage, relished her belle-of-the-ball status in the all-male environment.

In the summer of 1945, when the corporal shipped out without proposing to Davis, the actress was besieged by fresh doubts about her attractiveness. She sequestered herself in Laguna Beach, where she soon grew weary of exchanging letters with Riley and, as she put it, *living in a mailbox*.[171] It was during a rare sortie to a local party that October that she met Sherry, a brawny ex-sailor and sometime painter who charmed the international superstar by asking what she did for a living. In her impatience to forget Riley's snub, Davis plunged into her most passionate affair since Farnsworth's death two years earlier. She met her mother's objections to the whirlwind romance with accusations of snobbery – so what if her beau's mother was an elevator operator in San Diego and his late father a carpenter? – and demolished the damning report on Sherry's past from Ruthie's private investigator. Her friends' warnings about Sherry's gold-digging motives likewise went unheeded.

Davis took her suitor on a spur-of-the-moment road-trip to Mexico City, where, in late November, just over a month after their first meeting, she and William Grant Sherry were married. Early in their honeymoon, Sherry hurled a trunk across the hotel room at his bride, and soon afterwards ejected her from the car, abandoning her by the side of the road. Even after the wedding, Sherry continued to insist that he had mistaken Davis for a local talent at the Laguna Beach community centre – not that he was ever much impressed by the extent of her fame. Once back in California, the blushing bride organised a private Bette Davis film festival to enlighten her new husband, but he had trouble staying awake through the presentation. 'I never liked the person that she was on screen,' he said. 'I always enjoyed the men in her pictures better, and her I just put out of my mind.'[172]

'She was the breadwinner, and I was the housewife,' Sherry said of their modern arrangement. 'I have dinner ready for her when she gets home. I take off her shoes and bring her slippers and a drink. I press her dresses when her maid isn't here and draw her bath and give her massages. I feel it's a privilege to do things for her.'[173] More interested in weight-lifting and sun-tanning than scrubbing and boiling, Sherry took on these menial household tasks only to thwart Ruthie's never-ending interference in the minutiae of her daughter's life. Inevitably, though, even a mental lightweight like Sherry would figure out that it wasn't her mother, but her work, that dominated Davis.

Davis seemed committed to her marriage in early 1947, when she requested maternity leave and spent a quiet winter with her husband in New England. There, on May Day of 1947, Davis gave birth by Caesarean section to Barbara Davis Sherry. Declaring the newborn's name – which was also her sister's – hopelessly dowdy, Davis soon shortened it to 'BD'. Davis rhapsodized that *I had no desire to give up my career, but somehow it didn't matter so much . . . I had had my Matterhorn. Now I was satisfied to be nestled in my little chalet.*[174] But for all her professed delight with her new role, the actress returned to Hollywood only three months after giving birth, hungry for the camera.

During Bette Davis's brief and tranquil seclusion, Ruthie and Bobby Davis were experiencing somewhat more violent transitions. In January of that year, Ruthie had separated from her husband of just over one year. Early in the summer of 1947, soon after BD's birth, Bobby got remarried, this time to David Berry, a drifter of 'imprecise occupation.'[175] Of her younger sister's conquest, Davis exclaimed, 'Now we're Mrs Sherry and Mrs Berry!' and upon learning that her new brother-in-law was a recovering alcoholic, shipped the newlyweds a dozen cases of liquor.[176]

Eighteen months later, Bobby sued her second husband for divorce on grounds of 'habitual intoxication' and returned to the psychiatric unit, where this time she stayed for two years.[177] Bobby never fully bounced back from this breakdown, and in the later years grew slavishly reliant on her sister.

Two years later, it was not domestic contentment that drove Davis back inside her little chalet, but her break-up with Jack Warner. The deluge of marvellous scripts the proud freelancer had anticipated never arrived. The few that trickled in were all, as Sherry remembered, 'just terrible stuff'.[178] Edgy and bitter, Davis sought distraction by pestering Sherry about his laziness, his parasitism and his inability to hold down a job. Sherry responded with regular beatings, and within just two months of leaving Warners Davis was equally ready to leave her third husband.

'That girl and I were made for each other, and I'm not going to let her go,' Sherry declared to reporters in October of 1949, after Davis had bundled up her infant daughter and secured a temporary restraining order against him. 'The whole trouble is due to my violent temper,' he went on. 'It's hooked up with the war, I think.'[179] This well-broadcast prostration won Davis back for a time. Sherry pelted her with a silver ice-bucket within days of their reconciliation, but Davis still stuck around for most of the spring. It was only in April of 1950, during an impromptu celebration of her 42nd birthday on the soundstage of her new film, *Payment on Demand* – the first decent project she had been offered in the eight empty months since *Beyond the Forest* – that Davis acted decisively on her frustration. In the midst of the festivities, Sherry stormed the set, accused Davis's co-star of cuckolding him and initiated a fistfight. Davis was furious: Sherry could wreck her body, but he couldn't touch her comeback. She left him for good.

That same month, just as the actress hit bottom in both her personal and professional lives, she received a telephone call from Darryl Zanuck – the first time the head of Twentieth Century Fox

Davis as Margo Channing in *All About Eve*. Unhappily her life imitated her art in this film, but if she noticed she made sure that it did not show

had made contact since chastising her for resigning as president of the Academy a decade before. Zanuck still disliked Davis, and only desperation brought about the surprising détente. Joseph Mankiewicz's *All About Eve* was set to go into production within weeks, and the film's slated star, Claudette Colbert, had broken her back on a skiing holiday in Switzerland. After various disagreements eliminated his preferred stand-ins – first Ingrid Bergman and then Marlene Dietrich – Zanuck with great reluctance nominated Davis for the lead. Putting his grudge aside, even Zanuck could see how appropriate Davis was for the role of Margo Channing, an ageing theatre legend confronting the terrors of middle age. Davis devoured Mankiewicz's screenplay (which is still considered the most brilliant send-up of the theatre in Hollywood history) in a single sitting, and declared it the wittiest and most intelligent script she had ever read. Whether or not she detected the similarities between herself and Margo Channing, Davis agreed to do the part the very next morning and only ten days later took the train to San Francisco to begin shooting her 61st film.

I detest cheap sentiment proclaims Margo – 'the kind of dame who would treat her mink coat like a poncho' – at the beginning of the picture: just the sort of sweeping condemnation Bette Davis was prone to issue. And just as Davis had unquestioningly succumbed to William Grant Sherry's smooth talk and biceps, so Margo Channing falls for the adulation of Eve Harrington (Anne Baxter), a mousy Midwesterner who professes to worship the older actress. Margo engages her young admirer as secretary and resident sycophant only to discover that Eve is no doe-eyed naïve but a ruthless megalomaniac, a girl who would 'ask Abbott to give her Costello'. As her protégée's nastiness surfaces, so do Margo's insecurities about her age, her staying power, her popularity, her femininity and her sex appeal.

Meeting Mankiewicz for the first time, Davis apologised for the huskiness of her voice, fallout from her final row with Sherry, whom she had left only a fortnight earlier. The director, however, was delighted with Davis's rasp; he later said that 'her snort and her laugh – both should be protected by copyright.'[180] Mankiewicz also predicted that his star's gravelly rumble would invite profitable comparisons to Tallulah Bankhead, said to be the real-life inspiration for Margo Channing. In any event, Mankiewicz was far more worried about Davis's personality than her voice. 'She will come to the stage with a thick pad of long yellow paper,' Edmund Goulding, who had directed Davis four times during her glory years, had cautioned. 'And pencils. She will write.'[181]

But though a criticism levelled at Margo – 'When will the

piano realise that it has not written the concerto?' – had applied all too well to Davis in the past, Davis surprised Mankiewicz by treating him with almost exaggerated respect from the beginning to the end of *All About Eve*. After years of delaying and endangering her films, Davis completed her stint as Margo Channing in just under a month.

Gary Merrill, the simian actor cast as Margo Channing's younger lover, Bill, deserved most credit for Davis's sudden softening. Unutterably dejected – grappling, as she put it, with *another divorce, my permanent need for love, my aloneness* – when she arrived in San Francisco, Davis was exhilarated by the attentions of Merrill, who was eight years her junior.[182] Of his own 'magnetic' attraction, Merrill said that his 'feeling of compassion for this misunderstood, talented woman was quickly replaced by a robust attraction . . . uncontrollable lust'.[183] In the film, Margo Channing's obsession with Eve's treachery threatens to poison even her relationship with Bill. Davis and Merrill encountered no such obstacles. The two launched into a loud boisterous affair, and soon Merrill, at a dinner party in the presence of his first wife, announced, 'I'd marry Bette Davis in a heartbeat if she'd have me.'[187] No matter if Davis was talking as much about Gary Merrill as Margo Channing when she proclaimed that *no project from the outset was as rewarding from the first*

Marilyn Monroe (1926–1962), in her cameo as the graduate of the Copacabana School of Dramatic Art, gave one of the finest performances of her early career in *All About Eve*. Davis, however, was not impressed. *That little blonde slut can't act her way out of a paper bag! She thinks if she wiggles her ass and coos, she can carry her scene. Well, she can't.*[184] In a more generous mood, Davis said that she felt at once Monroe would become a star. *She was very handsome. None of the men were interested in her at all, which was fascinating. I just thought she was very clever. She sat on the set reading Dostoevsky. Which was of course ridiculous.*[185] *Poor thing,* she went on, *nobody imagined that she would become a star. A nervous breakdown – that seemed inevitable.*[186]

'Fasten your seatbelts it's going to be a bumpy night,' Bette Davis warns guests, most pointedly the young Marilyn Monroe, in the most celebrated scene in *All About Eve* 1950

day to last as *All About Eve*; the film turned out marvellously.[188]

'Hollywood's most thrilling comeback in 1950 was made by its finest actress,' Hedda Hopper wrote of Davis as Margo, going on to observe that a 'succession of bad pictures had proved that not even the queen was immune to the skids.'[189] Said another critic, 'Bette Davis, for nearly two decades one of our greatest actresses and worst performers, finally is shaken out of her tear-jerking formula and demonstrates what a vivid, overwhelming force she possesses.'[190] This is Davis's greatest accomplishment in *Eve*: even if she had to play herself to do so, for the first time in several years she gave a breathtaking performance.

Among the film's 14 Oscar nominations (a record matched only in 1998 by *Titanic*), Davis received her eighth for Best Actress. Success seemed so certain that she scarcely even griped when her co-star Anne Baxter successfully fought for a nomination in the same category, and she and Davis became the first actresses in Hollywood history to be nominated in the same category for the same film. Unfortunately, as the director later explained, 'Bette lost *because* Annie was nominated. Annie lost *because* Bette Davis ditto.'[191] Once again, Davis's third Oscar was denied her. In life as in art, the scheming understudy had stolen the great star's thunder.

Perhaps another Eve Harrington overlap occurred that summer, when William Grant Sherry, only recently divorced from Davis, announced his engagement to Marion Richards, the 21-year-old former nanny to Davis's daughter, BD. The circumstances were by no means identical: Richards was an au pair, not an understudy, and Davis's love for Sherry had already perished, whereas Margo's for Bill was fresh and passionate. Still, what Margo Channing feared most in *Eve* – losing not just her career, but her lover, to a younger woman – had befallen Bette Davis in real life. Richards believed that it was Davis's humiliation over Sherry's union that impelled her to rush into marriage for the fourth time. 'Bette pushed Gary into it,' Marion Richards explained. 'She was saving face. She didn't want it to look like her husband had thrown her away for a young girl.'[192] Whatever the impetus, on 28 June 1950, only three months after meeting Merrill (and the same day that his own divorce was finalised), Davis headed back to Mexico and said her wedding vows for the fourth and last time in a quickie ceremony in Juarez.

Davis offered a different explanation for her decision to tie the knot again with such haste. *I sensed in Gary my last chance at love and marriage*, she said of her *coup de foudre* passion. *I wanted these as desperately as ever.*[193] She had always sworn off dating fellow thespians, but Merrill, at last, seemed a man worth taking seriously, and he had come along at a propitious point in her life. Like her alter ego Margo Channing, Davis had long been divided between the demands of work and 'life', a struggle that Margo shelves in the most famous monologue in *All About Eve*:

Funny business, a woman's career. The things you drop on the way up the ladder so that you can move faster – you forget you'll need them again when you go back to being a woman. That's one career all females have in common whether we like it or not. Being a woman . . . and in the last analysis nothing is any good unless you can look up just before dinner, or turn around in bed, and there he is. Without that, you're not a woman. You're something with a French provincial office, or a book full of clippings. But you're not a woman. Slow curtain. The end.

Ending with *fame and fortune aren't worth a thing without a man to come home to*, Margo's speech champions the anti-feminist ethos of the post-war era, condemning hard-boiled careerists like Eve Harrington to loneliness and rank misery. This retrograde message, which doubtless helped make *All About Eve* the first Bette Davis picture to attract equal numbers of men and women, held particular significance for the actress at the age of 42. After marrying Merrill, she had begun to entertain visions of a quiet countryside cottage, fresh-baked pie and yowling offspring: Margo's response to ageing seemed to have its merits. But

Margo Channing was not a bitch, Davis was still insisting in 1973. *She was an actress who was getting older and was not too happy about it. And why should she be? Anyone who says that life begins at forty is full of crap. As people get older their bodies begin to decay. They get sick. They forget things. What's good about that?*[194]

before going the Margo Channing route into the domestic sunset, Davis did her damnedest to have it all: the man and the marquee, the family and the fame.

In 1950, it almost seemed as if Davis would succeed. In fewer than three months, she had divorced, fallen in love all over again, delivered what was arguably the finest performance of her career and remarried. That summer, she even dipped her appendages into the pavement of Hollywood Boulevard, a tribute many thought long overdue. *There is a near-perfect time in a person's life*, Davis said, *just past 40, when you have outgrown most of the wildness, either the work is going well or you have adjusted your sights, and you are at peace with your private self. The time may come only once, and this was mine.*[195]

Bette Davis was a star not a wife and, as it turned out, even less of a mother. In countless fan interviews in the past, she had disdained what she called the *maternal type* and, more emphatically, claimed that *I could never adopt a child because I would have to feel that the child belonged to me, was my own flesh and blood or not at all.*[196] In the early 1950s, however, Davis changed her mind and cajoled Merrill into starting a family with her. He agreed to adopt a baby, requesting only that they first get a boy to balance out Davis's daughter by her third marriage, BD. Davis soon brought home a girl, named Margot after Davis's character in *Eve*, with a 't' thrown in to differentiate flesh from fiction. A year and a half later, to placate her husband, Davis adopted a boy, Michael, as well. To complete the brood, the actress's biological daughter,

Playing at the fifties idyll, the Merrill family, Bette and Gary with her daughter Barbara and their adoptive children Margot and Michael

BD, three when her mother remarried, changed her surname from Sherry to Merrill.

Despite these efforts at domesticity, Davis still very much doubted that 'real' women choose love over ambition and intimacy over acclaim. Many had called her more than human, so why couldn't she have both? In the wake of *Eve*, her career seemed to be growing in tandem with her family. But both triumphs were brief. Problems with her 'last chance' at love and marriage surfaced as early as the couple's honeymoon, a cross-country drive to New England: *An hour after I married him*, Davis admitted much later, *I knew I had made a terrible mistake.*[197] Their differences in temperament proved incompatible and even incendiary. Where Merrill was laid-back and easy-going, Davis was highly-strung and all-controlling, and though she held his New England pedigree – his family dated back to the *Mayflower* – in high esteem, she resented her new husband's lack of motivation, his readiness to ascribe his success to good looks and wealthy parents. *Suddenly I was interested in* his *career*, Davis said. *I was growing tired of mine.*[198] Later, expanding on the subject: *I had seen Hollywood marriages fail, when the husband's career is in the doldrums and the wife's is hot – or vice versa.*[199]

'I've always had a casual approach to life,' Gary Merrill said in an interview about his memoir, *Bette, Rita, and the Rest of My Life*, published in 1989. 'I sort of float along. I wanted to get through everything as easily as possible. Maybe I'm a child at heart. Bette is a perfectionist. I'm lazy. I wear the same old clothes. She likes change. She would never play golf because she didn't play well. I played and never cared what people thought of my game. We even disagreed about raising our children. My theory about children is to treat them like people. You can't look down on them and say: "Do this! Do that!" She treated our kids like a master sergeant. We're people,' Merrill concluded, 'of two extremes.'[200]

Davis's sure-fire comeback after *All About Eve* proved also to be

As with all of her marriages romance was followed by anger and disillusion, her fourth and last, to Gary Merrill, lasted the longest

a mirage. The more futilely Davis sweated for parts, the more her husband's laissez-faire attitude to movie making grated on her. By early 1951, Davis had received so few offers that she had no choice but to trail Merrill to England to star opposite him in *Another Man's Poison*. Bitter at having landed the part only because she happened to be married to the star, Davis raised hell during their three-month stay in England, tormenting her husband and baiting her colleagues by ostentatiously dining on steaks that she had shipped from the States. In post-war Britain, where meat was still strictly rationed, Davis was castigated in the tabloids for her extravagance. The movie, overshadowed by the sensational opening of *A Streetcar Named Desire* that same week, attracted considerably less attention. Davis, one reviewer wrote, played 'everything in a blaze of breath-taking absurdity. From beginning to end, there is not a life-like inflection, a plausible reaction. She does, in the cant phrase, The Lot.'[201] For her next job, *Phone Call From a Stranger*, Davis was forced to accept another tag-along part – this one much smaller – from her husband.

Things took a promising turn when she was offered the meaty lead in *The Star*, a 'Hollywood insider' sizzler written by an ex-employee of Joan Crawford, about a pathetic and alcoholic has-been actress reduced to working as a department-store clerk. Davis was so eager to lampoon her detested rival that she failed to notice how much her own personality also corresponded to that of the fictional former actress, Margaret Elliot. But Margaret Elliot was no Margo Channing, lacking as she did all nobility and complexity, all charisma and sympathy. Elliot echoed only the worst, most embarrassing experiences of Davis's middle age: her decline in popularity and concomitant obsession with making a come-back; her imperious rejection of 'tripe' forced on her by producers; her inability to adapt her persona to her age; her superhuman willpower; and her undisguised sexual desperation. *The Star* did poorly at the box office, but to the wonderment of many, her role as Margaret Elliot earned Davis her ninth Academy Award nomination. By this point, however, few regarded Bette Davis as a serious contender. To all who mattered in Hollywood, Bette Davis was all too similar to Margaret Elliot on the fateful night that she takes her beloved Academy Award on a drunken bender, roaring 'C'mon, Oscar, let's you and I get drunk!' After *The Star*, film offers stopped altogether.

I love Hollywood, Davis continued to aver even after Hollywood no longer seemed to return the compliment. *The only reason anyone goes to Broadway is because they can't get work in the movies.*[202] She was even more emphatic, in early 1952, about her reasons for leaving California: *Actors always say, 'I am returning to the stage to refine my craft,' but that's a bunch of BS. No one leaves the movies for the stage unless they can't get work. And I'm no exception.*[203] Still, though she held the theatre in open contempt, that spring Davis had no choice but to settle for the lead in the Ogden Nash stage musical *Two's Company*. She moved her young family to Manhattan to prepare for her first stage appearance in 22 years.

Davis was less lithe and far less compliant than when she had last appeared on Broadway, a quarter-century before. She flubbed her song-and-dance routines in the *Two's Company* rehearsals, but rather than work to improve her performance, she complained that *the ballet became a far more important adjunct to the show than its star*.[204] Surrounded by a brigade of lackeys, she imperiously ignored the director's every suggestion. Then, at the first preview performance in October, while waiting to make her entrance by popping out of a box, Davis, overtaken by dizziness, momentarily lost consciousness. Though she revived in time for her cue, seconds later she thudded headfirst on to the stage and blacked out. Experiencing extreme fatigue after this strange accident, Davis consulted Dr Max Jacobson, the notorious 'Dr Feelgood' who administered so-called 'vitamin injections' to the crème de la crème of mid-century America, keeping luminaries as diverse as JFK, Sammy Davis Jr, and Judy Garland awake with high dosages of amphetamines.

When *Two's Company* opened in New York that December, it was to decidedly negative notices, most of which focused on its star's limited repertoire; one reviewer compared Davis's descent from the 'Parnassus' of serious acting to 'listening to Beethoven's Fifth played on a pocket comb'.[205] This critical scorn fast penetrated the fog induced by Dr Feelgood's doses of amphetamines, and Davis sought the advice of a real doctor, who informed her that Jacobson's injections, in numbing her pain, had concealed a serious illness, osteomyelitis of the jaw, the same sort of bacterial infection that had afflicted Ruthie 30 years earlier. Half of Davis's jaw was removed in a lengthy operation that the actress later associated with the onset of her *ten black years*,[206] and she bowed out of *Two's Company* after only 89 performances, refusing to answer charges that she had orchestrated the medical escape route.

Instead, Davis turned her energies to the domestic stage, investing her hefty insurance hand-out in a rambling clapboard house in rural Maine – 'Witch-Way', she called it – where the actress swore off professional engagements to embrace the role that had always attracted her least, that of the 'dutiful country wife'.[207] She was soon flinging as much energy into being a wife as she once had into being a star. She oversaw the planting of fruit trees, the slaughtering of sheep and the gathering of lobsters. She mingled with the local PTA, led expeditions into the sub-zero surf to fortify her loved ones' immune systems, and even tried her hand at down-home cooking, piling nutritious seaweed pudding on her children's dinner plates.

Soon enough, the Merrills stood out in the small rural community less for their fame than for their bizarre lifestyle. Chauffeurs, gardeners, housekeepers and au pairs, none of whom stayed long, whispered about Merrill's habit of strolling naked into the kitchen to mix pre-dawn martinis, and Davis's obsessive-compulsive housekeeping. The couple's adopted daughter, Margot, whose angelic blondeness had assumed a menacing aspect at Witch-Way, also excited considerable gossip. While Davis had always applauded BD's temper tantrums, judging them evidence of the girl's fiery inheritance, Margot's conduct suggested something rather bleaker: the three-year-old howled and wailed for nights on end, often stripped off her clothing, and caressed herself in public. Once she even tried to strangle a cat, but it was only after her violence extended to the infant Michael that the Merrills took action. They confined Margot to an attic bedroom and then a straitjacket, before finally taking her to the doctor.

Margot was diagnosed with serious brain damage. Her IQ would never exceed 60. 'I was very depressed,' Merrill said of the doctor's findings. 'I can't remember if I cried. I felt like it. All I thought was: "We have a problem, a problem, a problem."'[208] When Ruthie Davis heard the news, she insisted that the Merrills return the toddler to the adoption agency as 'damaged goods'.[209] Davis's husband, still a devoted father, resisted at first, engaging a full-time nurse to monitor Margot, but he soon had no choice to preserve the peace but to place Margot in the Lochland School. She was to live in this mental health institution for more or less the rest of her life.

Margot's departure did little to improve life at Witch-Way. In her scandalous 1985 memoir, *My Mother's Keeper*, BD remembers her mother during those years as restless and bored and Merrill as mean-spirited and alcoholic; husband and wife fought for their children's allegiances, with Davis's adoration of BD increasing in direct proportion to her hatred of Merrill, who in turn courted his son to alienate Davis. To shift Michael's sympathies back into her camp, Davis began to stage suicide attempts, a custom that, according to BD, she never gave up for the rest of her life.

Although Merrill spent most of the year travelling to work on films, his infrequent homecomings brought not celebration but catastrophe. Davis habitually summoned the police with complaints of her husband's physical abuse, but BD believed that Merrill's taunts hurt far more than his fists. Merrill ridiculed his wife's has-been status, regularly chucking her two Oscars at her and once even pressing the cherished statuettes into the hands of a puzzled cabbie. From this behaviour Davis deduced that *he wanted Margo Channing, not a little wife and mother*. Merrill, Davis concluded, *was disappointed that I didn't keep more of a star image in my private life. He didn't want me to be in the kitchen. He didn't approve of my domestic streak.*[210]

Davis in turn was enraged when Merrill retired from films between 1954 and 1960, if only because she and her husband had never managed to limit their superstar lifestyles to meet the financial demands of three children: BD, a devoted equestrienne, required private lessons and the maintenance of her own horse; Michael, the training afforded by exclusive private schools; and Margot, the ministrations of Lochland's staff. Three years after making *The Star*, Davis made several pictures in Hollywood, all of them flops.

In 1957, Davis left Merrill — who, as BD remembered, 'came close to killing Mother a few times' that year – at Witch-Way to pursue work in California, but she just barely scraped out an income with guest slots on television shows. She began to wonder if perhaps she had taken her Hausfrau shtick too seriously at Witch-Way. She had become, she said, a *psychotic eater* who grew frumpier with every home-brewed stew.[212] *Now 40 is not much at all, and everyone exercises and everyone has plastic surgery and eats right. We did none of that. I certainly didn't, and by 45, I did not look that wonderful.*[213]

She embarked on a crash diet, for which she was soon rewarded with the lead in a stage adaptation of *Look Homeward, Angel*, but no sooner had rehearsals started than Davis, exploring the Merrills' new Los Angeles home one afternoon,

I went back to work because someone had to pay for the groceries, Davis said in 1955.[211]

In 1956, Davis returned to work in the film *The Virgin Queen*, in which she played Queen Elizabeth again. Her adopted son Michael, who had never seen his mother act before, at first had trouble understanding her transformation when he went to see her filming her second film about Elizabeth I, *The Virgin Queen*. On his first visit to the soundstage, Michael tugged at Gary Merrill's wrist, confused to see Bette screaming at the actor playing Sir Walter Raleigh. 'Daddy,' he asked, 'Why is Mommy mad at that man instead of you?'[214]

mistook a dark stairwell for a closet and plummeted ten feet into the cellar. She emerged with a concussion and a severely bruised spine, and soon became deeply depressed. The injury forced her to drop out of the play and her physical condition came to symbolise her powerlessness over other aspects of her life. Rattled, Davis called it quits on her fourth marriage, but soon realised that she was unable to *face being alone again*,[215] and reconciled with Merrill in late 1957.

The couple went on holiday in Florida without their children and when this failed to improve their relations, they tried distance. In the summer of 1958, with her sister and 11-year-old daughter in tow – the 'Three B's' – Bette sailed for Europe, leaving her husband and son in Maine. The two movies that Davis made in Europe rank among the worst performances of her career, and when she returned home in 1959, she was more eager than ever to patch up her marriage. She agreed to collaborate onstage with Merrill in a nationwide tour of *The World of Carl Sandburg*, a tribute to the venerable Midwestern poet and social critic. Davis had high hopes for the unusual project, a staged dramatic reading of Sandburg's work, which afforded an auspicious opportunity to manage creative, marital, and financial problems all at once. But though the husband-wife team wowed audiences in the 72 cities that they visited, there was no applause backstage. Before the final dress rehearsal, Davis had moved out of the house, and throughout the long tour never once shared a hotel room with her husband – not even in San Francisco, when they ended up at the same establishment where their romance had sparked during the making of *Eve*.

A few days before *The World of Carl Sandburg* was scheduled to open on Broadway, Merrill was fired. Davis it seemed, had gone to the producers and forced them to choose between the two of them. This betrayal decided Merrill, and he left the marriage for good. The show soon collapsed without him, and he embarked on a rebound affair with Rita Hayworth, an actress Davis had always despised for her beauty. To revenge herself, Davis took drastic measures to cut Merrill off from his children – particularly Michael, whose obvious preference for his father had always rankled. In a series of eight lawsuits aimed at denying Merrill formal visitation rights, Davis railed against her ex-husband for *excessive drinking, physical cruelty, and irresponsibility.*[216]

She claimed that vacations with him would upset their school schedules and his alcoholic rages would endanger their lives. She even went so far as to argue that that his Malibu beach house – where the family had all lived together – was an *unsuitable abode* for young people.[217]

Bette with Barbara 1957

Impoverished by these custody hearings – all of which she herself had initiated – Davis entered the 1960s so desperate for money that she took up a publisher's long-standing offer to publish her autobiography. She settled into her Upper East Side townhouse with ghostwriter Sanford Dody, who found the actress to be evasive and dishonest about the details of her past. Davis's blurry memory worsened considerably after Ruthie Davis died of coronary thrombosis in the summer of 1961. On her deathbed, Ruthie demanded a coffin made of pure silver from her daughter. Davis, though at the time weathering her worst financial difficulties to date, still felt she owed Ruthie her professional success, and indulged her mother's last request.

While irritated that her mother's extravagances persisted even in death, in public Davis fanned her grief. When Dody showed Davis his draft, the actress excised all even remotely negative references to her dearly departed mother, which the ghostwriter had considered among the book's most powerful passages. In other arenas, too, Davis used *The Lonely Life* to soothe her conscience, turning her apologia into a direct personal attack on her fourth and last husband. Adept at playing the victim, Davis put all the blame on Merrill for the failure of their marriage: *I am sure I have been uncompromising, peppery, intractable, monomaniacal, tactless, volatile and oftentimes disagreeable*, she wrote, *I stand accused of it all. But at 40 I allowed the female to take over, and it was too late. I admit that Gary broke my heart. He killed the dream forever. The little woman no longer exists.*[218]

Davis was more than willing to consign mentally ill Margot to her drunken, reckless ex-husband. Even after moving to Connecticut in the 1960s to live near BD, Davis showed almost no interest in Margot. When she remembered to fetch Margot for her scheduled vacations from Lochland, Davis interpreted her adopted daughter's slowness as a defect of personality, not cerebrum. Insisting on treating Margot like an equal, Davis lashed out whenever Margot disappointed or 'disobeyed' her. Finally, in 1965 Davis granted Merrill full custody of Margot, and seldom saw her after the early 1970s. Until his death in 1990, Merrill alone footed Margot's hospital bills.

Much later, Davis wrote that *I knew long ago, even before I titled my book* The Lonely Life *that I would wind up alone.*[219] She explained on many other occasions: *If I'd been a little B-actress, or better yet, not an actress at all, I might have found that one special someone to stay with all my life.*[220] Through all her lonely decades, she held on to her belief that *an actress ultimately has to choose between giving up the man or the career. And really, men do come and go, but as long as one can work, one is fine. In the final analysis, work is all there is.*[221]

What happens, in that case, when all the work disappears?

Bette-Davis-is-Bette-Davis-is-Bette-Davis • 1960–1989

THIS WASTED BERNHARDT

In early 1962, Bette Davis placed a peculiar advertisement in Hollywood trade journals:

Mother of Three – 10, 11, and 15 – divorcee, American. Thirty years' experience as an actress in motion pictures. Mobile still and more affable than rumour would have it. Wants steady employment in Hollywood. (Has had Broadway.) Bette Davis. References on request.[222]

This posting brought Davis more attention than she had received in a decade, but it was not of the type she might have craved. On the contrary, Davis was excoriated for the gesture, which most interpreted as evidence of her self-destructive streak – and her arrogance and rancour. For all the insults, though, few claimed to understand Davis's precise reasons for advertising her desperation in such a way. Was it a joke? A suicide mission? In vain Davis tried to dismiss it as *facetious* and *sardonic*; the damage to her reputation had been done.[223]

By any reckoning, the last few years had been hard on Davis. Her downwards spiral into box-office oblivion seemed unstoppable. In the last years of her marriage to Gary Merrill, she had made several attempts at professional resurrection, all catastrophic. In 1956 she reprised her once-popular Queen Elizabeth role in *The Virgin Queen*, but she was alone in appreciating how much better her advanced age suited her regal subject; audiences reacted with indifference. That same year, in *Storm Center*, Davis played a priggish small-town librarian fighting to keep *The Communist Dream*, a text local doyens deemed dangerous for its Marxist sympathies, on the shelves. It was this film that most emphasised how out of touch Davis had become with the temper of Hollywood and, for that matter, the rest of America. *Storm Center*'s bland dialogue and formulaic storyline failed to disguise its inappropriate theme. Released too soon after the inflammatory anti-Communist investigations of the House Un-American Activities Committee, the film did little more than stoke the anxieties of Red-fearing citizens across the land and diminish Davis's popularity all the more. Following another ill-realised role as a Bronx housewife in *The Catered Affair* (also in 1956), Davis did not embark on another major project until after her divorce from Merrill, in 1961. She had enormous hopes for Frank Capra's *A Pocketful of Miracles*, in which she was cast as Apple Annie, a homeless apple vendor with a knack for bringing gangsters good

Davis reprised her role as Elizabeth I in The Virgin Queen 1956

luck. *A Pocketful of Miracles* was a story typical of the rags-to-riches morale-boosters that had been immensely popular during the Great Depression, but – as both Capra and Davis understood too late – that genre of parable held little interest for the prosperous movie-goers of the 1960s. The picture bombed.

After this string of disappointments, Davis's next undertaking marked something of a nadir: professionally, personally and even psychologically. She had accepted a minor role in the world premiere of Tennessee Williams's new play, *The Night of the Iguana*, telling the show's producers – who expressed concerns about Davis's reputation – that *I would rather have the third part in a Tennessee Williams play than a lead in an ordinary play.*[224] As Williams knew perfectly well, Bette Davis had never been much of an ensemble actress, and from the first rehearsal she plotted to shove her character, Maxine Faulk – an over-the-hill ex-seductress in denial about her advancing age and fading beauty – into the spotlight. Davis, it seemed, fed off the same pathetic fantasies as Williams's character – or so reckoned Patrick O'Neal, the lead actor 20 years her junior, when she propositioned him one night. Delusions of grandeur also plagued Davis, who sabotaged the rehearsals at every opportunity in the hope of augmenting her role. Then, at the preview of *The Night of the Iguana*, Davis tripped backstage. She attended the cast party intact that night, but the next morning rolled on to the set in a wheelchair 'suffering', in the words of one reporter, 'from a wrenched knee and a secondary part'.[225]

More and more, it was the actress's mental, not physical, condition that alarmed her colleagues. One afternoon, Williams and the play's director, Frank Corsaro, strolled into the empty theatre to see a figure hunched over on the stage, scrubbing the floor. They fell silent, identifying the creature as none other than Bette Davis: 'There she was, looking like a charwoman, with a pail of water and a mob, swabbing the floor,' Corsaro remembered, and

Whatever Happened to Baby Jane (1962) saw Davis cast against Joan Crawford, the actress she most detested.

later said that Davis 'represented something of the motion picture horror. The movies have created terrifying children who have become stars. Bette Davis's vanity was profound, and it had to be, because it masked a vulnerability that was just as profound.'[226]

At the play's Broadway opening, after fans greeted Davis's entrance with raucous whistling and caterwauling, the actress raised her arms in a prize-fighter's gesture and then, though it was nowhere in the script, held the Victory pose for several agonising minutes. Davis later justified her behaviour by saying that *the applause went on such a long time that I was forced to step out of character and bow. It was very unnerving.*[227] But as this *unnerving* enthusiasm diminished with every performance, so did Davis's endurance. In April 1962, upon learning that she was not even being considered for the film version, Davis demanded a release from her contract on familiar – only this time, beyond all doubt bogus – medical grounds. The producers soon consented, less because they believed her than because they had lost the will to haggle: Bette Davis, all were coming to agree, no longer merited the liability. After only 128 performances, Davis left the play with by then familiar promises never to return to the stage.

Davis's repeated consultations with doctors had generated a

great number of bills, and after the *Iguana* debacle she no longer had the paycheques to settle them. She was, then, in no position to turn down director Robert Aldrich's cash offer of $25,000 to star opposite her most despised contemporary, Joan Crawford, in the horror B-movie *Whatever Happened to Baby Jane?* Davis also doubtless relished the perversity of her character, Baby Jane Hudson, a former child star rotting in a dilapidated Hollywood mansion with her longsuffering older sister, Blanche, to be played by Crawford. As a child, Baby Jane enjoys a brief run of fame singing 'I've Written a Letter to Daddy' in vaudeville shows, but it is ultimately Blanche who becomes the movie star. *Whatever Happened to Baby Jane?* begins several decades after Blanche is crippled in a mysterious automobile accident that forces her to move in with, and depend entirely upon, the sister who hates her.

Communicating Baby Jane's

Joan Crawford (1904?–1977), a former chorus girl from Texas, epitomised the 'flapper movement' on film, in the 1920s, then became one of the few actresses to survive the transition from silents to talkies. Frequently paired with Clark Gable on the screen, Crawford stayed at the glamorous studio MGM for the same length of time that Davis was at Warners, 18 years. In 1943, Crawford signed with Warners, and began appearing in the kinds of roles that were less and less frequently offered to Davis. But despite her 1945 Oscar victory for *Mildred Pierce*, Crawford came to suffer from the same fading-star problems that dogged Bette Davis. It was only in 1974, when she failed to recognise herself in a magazine snapshot, that Crawford decided to retire from public life altogether. From then until her death in 1977, Crawford focused on Christian Science, vodka, and the four adopted children she had long since alienated.

resentment came easily to Davis, who had loathed Crawford, coining some of her finest one-liners at her co-star's expense. Davis once declared of Crawford: *She's slept with everyone on the MGM lot except Lassie*, and on another occasion *Why am I so good at playing bitches? I think it's because I'm not a bitch. Maybe that's why Miss Crawford always plays ladies.*[228] Of her experience working with Crawford on the film, Davis quipped, *The best time I had working with Joan Crawford was when I pushed her down the stairs.'*[229] Davis had disliked Crawford since the start of her career: as early as 1936, when told of her rival's plans to act in a Shakespeare play, Davis purred, *How wonderful. We are all so thrilled that Joan has learned to read.*[230] From the beginning, entertainment writers were rabidly curious about the stars' sour relationship, later the subject of an entire book, *Bette and Joan: The Divine Feud*. In public statements Davis denied any outright conflict (*I hated her guts, but we did not feud at all*), but she never hesitated to point out the differences between her and her co-star.[231] Despite her itinerant, fatherless upbringing, Davis came from fine New England stock, and had benefited from classical stage training. In contrast, Crawford – born Lucille Le Sueur in San Antonio, Texas – had clawed her way to fame via a series of strip bars and cabaret acts and well-situated lovers. And while both actresses had obsessive-compulsive tics, Davis restricted hers to the domestic sphere. *On Jane she wouldn't even shake hands with anyone,* Davis once seethed of Crawford's on-set behaviour. *She always carried disinfectants with her and she'd scrub the john on her hands and knees.*[232]

But beyond even her questionable background, insincerity and opportunism, it was Crawford's vanity that Davis claimed to find most irritating of all. Unlike Davis, who was only too willing to sacrifice her attractiveness for Baby Jane's derangement, Crawford refused to conform her appearance to Blanche's invalided condition, or, as Davis fumed, *She wouldn't give up the boobs. They kept getting bigger and bigger. She's supposed to be shrivelling away while Baby Jane starves her to death, but her tits keep* growing! *I keep running into them like the Hollywood Hills!*[233]

It was at this high tide of frustration that Davis placed her unfortunate job advertisement. She was uncommonly lucky that *Whatever Happened to Baby Jane?* was released so soon afterwards.

In just 11 days, *Baby Jane* earned $9 million and paid back its costs. With its sensational advertising ('Sister sister oh so fair, why is there blood all over your hair?' the movie posters read) promising the compelling wreckage of two of the Golden Age's most admired stars, *Baby Jane* was immensely popular. Popular enough, in fact, to rehabilitate Davis's reputation and spare her further ridicule – at least for the moment.

This surge in respect seems strange considering Davis's role in the movie. As Baby Jane

Baby Jane's budget was so low that, along with the $25,000 cash advance, Davis was promised a small percentage of the profits. Cannier or simply richer than her co-star, Crawford, who was married to the president of Pepsi-Cola at the time, accepted a smaller up-front fee in exchange for a larger profit share. For the rest of her life, Davis complained about how much more money Crawford ended up making from the project.

Hudson, Davis camped it up like never before. An absurd, macabre creation resembling an oversized Raggedy-Ann doll, Baby Jane – when she is not rehearsing her long-ago vaudeville hit, 'I've Written a Letter to Daddy' – for her comeback – spends her screen time serving her paralysed sister dead canaries and knocking off the domestic help. Davis claimed to be just as thrilled about the chance *Baby Jane* gave her daughter BD, then 15, who played a small part as the Hudsons' next-door neighbour in the film. Acting was a cinch for the coltish adolescent, who had shouldered many grown-up responsibilities since her stepfather's departure two years earlier.

The fact that the picture was a success is a miracle in my life, Davis said of the film. *Perhaps it was the great law of compensation for ten hellish years.*[234] In a less emotional mood, she told another reporter that *Everybody told {Aldrich} not to make a picture with two old broads.*[235] The next day, Davis received a telegram from Crawford that seemed to sum up all their differences: 'Please do not refer to me in that manner in the future.'[236]

Davis, unlike Crawford, claimed not to mind growing old: what riled her was fading from the public eye. *I would like always to be doing something, not just sitting back*, she said in a documentary made toward the end of her life. *I love to work, that is really my survival.*[237] She had none of the shrewdness of Greta Garbo, who retired into seclusion at the age of 36, while still beautiful and sought-after; still less did she sympathise with Crawford's brand of *striving-to-be-a-lady actresses who seemed terrified of not coming across as sympathetic.*[238] Davis would play any monster, as long as it allowed her to keep playing. When she received her first Academy Award nomination in a decade for *Baby Jane*, she was sure that the honour meant another comeback, another chance at the only life she knew how to lead.

When denied her third statuette once again, Davis blamed her failure on her co-star's interference, claiming that Crawford – devastated because she had received no nomination herself – actively campaigned against her co-star, then telephoned all the other nominees offering to accept the award for them if they were unable to attend the ceremony. (Crawford did exactly this for Anne Bancroft when she was announced as the winner. Davis said that she *nearly dropped dead.*[239]) Though Baby Jane still stands as the role that modern audiences most associate with her, except perhaps for Margo Channing, more discerning film critics believe that Davis's pride in this farce was misplaced, and that *Baby Jane* demonstrated nothing so much as how far she had fallen.

As with *All About Eve*, the sensational reception of *Whatever Happened to Baby Jane?* promised a great recovery that never materialised. Davis did indeed entertain a new flurry of offers, but the parts were not the sort that she, in her golden years, would have deigned to read, much less accept. In retrospect, it seems apposite that the release of *Baby Jane* coincided with Davis's act of desperation in the trade magazines, for this film – even more so than *Beyond the Forest* 13 years before – signalled the actress's decisive retreat into caricature. Over the next decade Davis would be pigeonholed as the one-eyed mother, the grotesque Gorgon, the drooling dowager, eroding into what *Time* magazine sneeringly called 'Hollywood's grand-dame ghoul'.[240] As the same magazine said of Davis's performance in the 1964 film *Dead Ringer*, another horror B-movie flop: 'Exuberantly uncorseted, her torso looks like a gunnysack full of galoshes. Coarsely cosmeticked, her face looks like a U-2 photograph of Utah. And her acting, as always, isn't really acting, it's shameless showing-off. But just try to look away.'[241]

Davis's only other role of even moderate significance in the 1960s was in *Hush, Hush . . . Sweet Charlotte* – so unrepentant a bid to rekindle *Baby Jane*'s box-office success that director Robert Aldrich originally called it *Whatever Happened to Cousin Charlotte?* In the beginning, he also insisted on reuniting the 'old broads' who had served him so well on *Baby Jane*. Still convinced that she had lost her third Oscar to Crawford's machinations, Davis had no more patience for her co-star, and it showed. On location in rural Louisiana, every night both stars called Aldrich in his hotel room: Crawford to whimper about Davis's unfriendliness, Davis to complain about the unacceptable size of Crawford's role. Even with the aid of her 'vodka life-support system', Crawford was soon so dispirited by Davis's rudeness that she fled to hospital with a vague respiratory complaint.[242] Crawford was listening to the radio from her hospital bed when she learned that Olivia de Havilland would be replacing her in the picture. (De Havilland had taken the role with great reluctance after several other actresses had turned it down. Vivien Leigh's refusal had been the most emphatic: 'I could just about look at Joan Crawford's face at 7 am on a Southern plantation,' she shuddered, 'but I could not possibly look at Bette Davis!')[243]

Davis's performance in what Pauline Kael called a 'Grand Guignol melodrama' entailed her 'crawling and howling and

Hush Hush Sweet Charlotte (1964) won little praise and much criticism for what were now considered to be her 'hag horror roles'

looking wildly repulsive'.[244] The role marked another stage in Davis's abandonment of serious acting. Kenneth Tynan was among the few to admire Davis as Charlotte, but even his praise for this 'raging, aging Southern belle; this wasted Bernhardt' had a distinctly elegiac ring, as if remembering a talent that had long since been extinguished.[245] The next year, in *The Nanny* – a lurid nursery-school thriller about a boy who suspects his au pair of having strangled his younger sister – Davis leered and teetered her way across the screen, camping it up on command.

'She was not unsuited to these subhorror films, but she was alien to their camp knowingness,' wrote film critic David Thomson. 'Her classic period had dealt with silly, overblown material, but she had always compelled audiences into sharing her belief in it. That faith was being modishly exploited in the sad spectacle of an actress submitting to a carpetbagger perversion of what was a rich and neurotic personality.'[246]

With every one of these 'hag horror roles' (Pauline Kael again), Davis was evolving from a figure of mystique and power into a laughing stock.[247] As early as 1958, one critic had tellingly commented: 'Bette-Davis-is-Bette-Davis-is-Bette-Davis, to crib from Gertrude Stein. Say that, and you've said it all.'[248] *The New York Times* would come to echo this sentiment, observing that 'Bette Davis – with her strident voice, nervous stride, mobile hands and popping eyes – is still her own best imitator.'[249] In her autobiography, Davis had said that *I was never completely Mildred or Hedvig or any other character. I was always Bette Davis watching herself become another person.*[250] By the 1970s, a popular comedian had a less generous spin on this phenomenon, and kicked off his Bette Davis act with the wisecrack, 'And now I would like to do a scene from all of my films.'[251]

In the 1970s – a decade in which Davis paid the bills with occasional cameo appearances in television shows like *Gunsmoke, Perry Mason* and *Wagon Train* (in which she almost always played herself), as well as several pilots that were never picked up – her only real success was backward-looking and reflective. In 1973, Davis toured America, then Europe and Australia, in a one-woman tribute to her own career. The first half of *The Bette Davis Show* featured clips from the films that had made her famous, drawn almost exclusively from her 18 years at Warners. With the exception of *Whatever Happened to Baby Jane?*, this section of the programme ignored all of Davis's projects after *All About Eve*, as if age 40 had not, in the end, been the actress's rebirth, but in fact her death. In the second part of the show, Davis appeared on stage to field pre-selected questions about her life in Hollywood. The show electrified its sold-out audiences, composed almost entirely of gay men, who had replaced single women as Davis's most loyal fans. In her extemporaneous ripostes, Davis displayed an unblemished, still razor-sharp wit, but her witty comebacks failed to conceal the discrepancy between her past greatness and her present desperation.

After her next and last stage venture, *Miss Moffat,* ended in reputation-damaging disaster, Davis retreated more and more into the nostalgia that *The Bette Davis Show* had exemplified, nursing and embellishing memories of loves and accolades long past just to survive each empty day. *I seem to keep re-enacting scenes from my movies!* she told an interviewer.[252] On and off the screen, she was feeding off stale memories: the present just couldn't compete.

GOD'S JOKE ON HUMANITY

After the break-up of her marriage to Merrill in 1960, Davis – who in the most famous one-liner in her autobiography dismissed sex as *God's joke on humanity* – swore off men for ever, or at least in newspaper articles about her.[253] *I am starting a campaign to do away with ALL men*, she told Hollywood columnist Hedda Hopper.[254] But though Davis never remarried, she spent her last years entangled with a series of much younger men, most of whom were either openly gay, or gold-diggers, or most frequently both. She had always attracted a large contingent of homosexual fans, who admired her for the same reasons that women during World War Two had: her fearlessness, her self-reliance, her outsider status, her constant struggle for acceptance.

As her pseudo-affairs ended time and again in disappointment – even after the actress proposed to some of her suitors – Davis concentrated her energies on her daughter BD, the only family member left to boss around, other than the ever-present Bobby. By the time she was a teenager, however, BD – who at 5'11" towered nine inches over her famous mother – felt as oppressed by these attentions as, a quarter of a century earlier, Davis had by Ruthie's.

In the summer of 1963, dutifully accompanying Davis to the Cannes Film Festival for the world premiere of *Baby Jane*, the 16-year-old BD met Jeremy Hyman, a 29-year-old Englishman whose uncle ran the Seven Arts Productions film company. They fell in love instantly, and the next month BD made ripples in the entertainment press when she announced her engagement to Hyman. The news floored her mother. Although Davis, unlike the overprotective and Puritanical Ruthie, had encouraged BD to date from the age of 12, the rapidity of Hyman's courtship had caught her completely off guard. Davis signed the parental consent forms only because she believed that the marriage would collapse within the year and BD would crawl back to her mother, more dependent than ever.

But BD had other ideas, telling reporters that 'Mummy's marriages don't reflect on mine for a large reason. She was a career woman, dedicated, even married to a career. I don't have that. I'm me. I've chosen the career of homemaker.'[257]

Davis not only scoffed at her daughter's self-description as a 'one-man woman'; she openly questioned BD's choice of man. (BD later alleged that Davis was hostile to Hyman not because of his personality or prospects but because he was English and half-Jewish.) Davis nevertheless provided BD with the most lavish of weddings on 4 January 1964. The month before, the devoted mother had even accepted a role in an abominable film, *Where Love Has Gone,* for the necessary $25,000 – the first time the actress ever admitted to taking a role exclusively for the money. Davis, who never ceased to remind BD of this sacrifice, was outraged to learn – from a press leak, no less – that, for tax purposes, BD and Hyman had already exchanged vows in a surreptitious civil ceremony in the last week of 1963.

This act of defiance set the precedent for all future dealings between Davis and her daughter. In the years following BD's

'Margo Channing, c'est moi!' was a rallying cry of gays' identification with Davis. A popular joke circulated Greenwich Village in the 1960s: 'You must be in love with Bette Davis, the way you go on about her!' a man says to his companion in a bar. 'In *love* with Bette Davis?' the companion replies. 'I *am* Bette Davis!'[255] Davis acknowledged her gay fan contingent with gratitude, but was careful to add that *I don't think it's fair to say it's because I'm flamboyant. I'm not flamboyant. In my personal life, I've never been known as flamboyant. Joan Crawford,* she couldn't resist drawing the contrast, *was flamboyant.*[256]

Posing together in 1964 beloved daughter Barbara was ultimately to cause Davis more pain than any other mortal with her cruel and badly written biography *My Mother's Keeper*

marriage, Davis made *Hush . . . Hush Sweet Charlotte* and *The Nanny*, but neither film came close to compensating for the loss of her beloved daughter. Rather than confront unemployment and isolation all at once, Davis relocated to Connecticut, purchasing a house two miles from the Hymans. The newly out-of-work actress swore that she had moved to keep an eye on her son Michael Merrill, a student in a nearby boarding school, but BD, from long experience, knew better.

BD by no means welcomed her mother's proximity, for at close range Davis disapproved all the more vigorously of Hyman, who had recently left the family film business to flirt with ill-defined entrepreneurial schemes. Shocked that a daughter of hers should while away her days darning socks and making pastries, Davis also issued some firm opinions about BD's new lifestyle, calling BD's servility disgusting and its recipient chauvinistic. Hyman, for his part, made no effort to conceal his distaste for his meddlesome mother-in-law. Davis felt entitled to her objections, because in spite of her ever-diminishing income, the Hymans lived almost entirely off her generosity for many years after their marriage. But while BD welcomed Davis's cash offerings, she refused her mother's extravagant gifts of clothing and jewellery, seeing them as a trap, just another means – like staging fake suicides, a Witch-Way habit that Davis re-embraced in Connecticut – of securing affection artificially. Still, BD was in no position to spurn all contributions. Hyman's get-rich-quick ventures – which included, to name only the most disastrous, a hay-hauling business – never lasted long, as BD's new husband visibly lacked his mother-in-law's work ethic.

When, after trying for five years, BD finally became pregnant in 1968, she and Hyman determined to exclude Davis from the delivery, and only invited the first-time grandmother to the hospital after BD had successfully given birth to a son, Ashley. Davis, who still claimed to love her daughter more than anything in the world, was stung by this gesture, especially as the rest of her domestic entourage was shrinking faster than her career. The same year that Ashley Hyman was born, Bette's sister Bobby – who had, since her last breakdown, served Davis as a *de facto* governess, housekeeper, and companion – packed up to join her daughter Fay's less demanding household in Arizona. With no Musketeer at her command, Davis hired a live-in personal assistant, Vik Greenfield, and thenceforth sent her sister in Phoenix $400 a month, a retirement pension for a lifetime of loyalty.

Greenfield – the most fired man in America, he jokingly

referred to himself – stayed with Davis off and on for the next eight years, an uneventful period in the actress's life, which she filled by returning to the useless bustle and the obsessive-compulsive routines of her childhood. Greenfield recalls Davis arranging and then rearranging crockery, cutlery, and canned goods several times a day; scrubbing the kitchen floor with even more frequency; and laying out ingredients for lunch 16 hours in

'My mother was just totally devoted to [Bette],' said Bobby's only daughter of the sibling relationship. '[Bobby] was a very passive type of person. My aunt was very dynamic. My mother worked for her and she tried to make everything peaceful in the house. My aunt was abusive to everybody. It wasn't just my mother. That's just the way Bette was.'[258]

advance. Oddly enough, though, for all this preoccupation with home maintenance, Davis gave personal hygiene no such attention: she seldom bathed, let alone washed her hair, more than once a week. Vodka came to replace lipstick in her beauty routine; if her daughter's testimony is at all accurate, Davis was seldom sober after 10 am in those years. 'She never found happiness, she never found fulfilment,' Greenfield said after Davis's death. 'She was, in my opinion, the unhappiest person I ever met'.[259]

Soon after Bobby's departure, Michael Merrill, during a vacation from boarding school, met and fell in love with Chou Chou Snow, a Connecticut neighbour. Fearful lest another child elope at the age of 16, Davis asked that Michael wait until his 21st birthday to marry Snow. In the summer of 1973, immediately after his college graduation, Merrill did exactly that, and later went on to become a perfectly respectable lawyer and lead a perfectly respectable adulthood in Boston. Davis behaved impeccably at the wedding, sitting next to her ex-husband and instigating not a single argument all day. The idyll's only blot was BD, who pleaded a 'prior commitment' and refused to attend the intimate ceremony.[260] More and more, BD was parading her scorn for her family with such gestures.

Davis, who had long depended on work to overcome personal hardships, found few distractions from BD's repeated rejections in the years between *The Nanny* (1965) and *The Bette Davis Show* (1973). The surge of hope that she experienced in early 1976, when she signed on to the TV movie *Burnt Offerings*, didn't last long, as Davis likened the slipshod production to *amateur night in Dixie*.[261] That same year, Davis had a far superior opportunity in another made-for-TV drama, *The Disappearance of Aimee*. But though initially excited about the project, she soon became pre-occupied with Faye Dunaway, whose mother Davis played in the film. Dunaway was the 'It' actress of the late 1970s; her ambition, allure, and potential resembled Davis's of 40 years before. As many had noted in the past, 'Davis could get along very well with co-workers who posed no threat, but she inevitably locked horns with actresses of her own stature.'[262] Consigning Dunaway to that sub-class of beautiful – and ergo insipid – actresses, Davis constantly attacked her co-star for arriving late for work, sulking in her dressing room, going on champagne sprees in limousines, and – most egregiously – having a part five times larger than her infinitely more 'professional' critic. Once Faye Dunaway, trying to be friendly, casually asked Davis what had changed since 'her day' in Hollywood. *This is my day,* the actress hissed in reply. *Legends do not date, lady.*[263]

Davis's mood improved on 1 March 1977 when she became the first woman ever to receive the American Film Institute's Lifetime Achievement Award. In a high-profile ceremony broadcast all over the country, Hollywood celebrities as diverse as Jane Fonda and William Wyler gave glowing speeches in Davis's honour. It was the actress's happiest night in years, a rapture punctured only by BD's refusal to attend.

The previous year, in 1976, the Hymans, hoping to wriggle free of Davis's constant interference in their lives, left Connecticut and bought a farmhouse in Pennsylvania. Davis refused to take the hint, however, and continued to pay her daughter frequent visits that were, in BD's words, 'not only uninvited by unwanted.'[264] Then, in August of 1977, BD dealt another blow to Davis when she gave birth, three weeks prematurely, to her second son, Justin Hyman, and once again failed to inform her mother beforehand. 'Do you want to see a scene from *Dark Victory* out in the lobby?' Hyman reportedly snarled when a nurse asked after his absent mother-in-law.[265] This slight did it for Davis: if she was no longer wanted in Connecticut, she would return to California and resume working – a move BD greeted with 'fantastic relief.'[266]

The aftermath of the American Film Institute tribute played no small part in Davis's abrupt 1978 decision to leave New England. The televised event had conferred a new vogue on the actress, as a new generation of filmmakers seemed to remember that this Golden Age legend wasn't dead yet. Back in Los Angeles, Davis – reminded anew that *my work has been the big romance in my life* – exulted in a deluge of film offers, working on back-to-back assignments for the first time since Warners.[267] Because she still preferred scripts to laurels, Davis hoped that the reprieve from the *flea-bitten, execrable, monstrously bad* roles of recent years would last this time; she even went so far as to imagine that her next picture, *Death on the Nile*, might bring her that ever-elusive third Academy Award.[268] The film was warmly received, but Davis's role as an uppity dowager who bullies paid companion Maggie Smith struck no critics as the stuff of Oscars. The next year, Davis did receive an Emmy (the TV equivalent of an Oscar) for *Strangers: the Story of a Mother and a Daughter*, a heart-warming – and, to Davis, quite familiar – story about an estranged family. But despite this institutional recognition, reviews of *Strangers*, which almost without exception saluted Davis as an 'institution' and a 'national treasure', suggested that the award was intended to celebrate not her performance, but her mere survival in the industry.[269]

Back in her West Hollywood apartment, Davis started drinking heavily again. As the film offers began to drop off once more, she grew so lonely that she begged her former hairdresser to move in with her, but that arrangement lasted only three months. Davis's misery intensified during her rare conversations with BD, who rejected outright all invitations to visit California. In 1979, Davis sought a replacement for her lost daughter. That June, the 71-year-old actress consulted the Yellow Pages and hired the 22-year-old Kathryn Sermak to accompany her to England, where she was slated to star in the Disney thriller, *The Watcher in the Woods*. A month later, en route to California after the shoot, Davis had just stopped off at the Hymans' Pennsylvania farm when she learned of Bobby's cancer-related death. Davis greeted the news with energetic despair, but the actress – who had already purchased a plot adjacent to Ruthie's for her sister – quickly regained enough presence of mind to veto Bobby's dying wish to be cremated. Davis did not attend her sister's funeral: no need, she declared, to draw attention away from Bobby in death as in life.

Without Kathryn Sermak at her side, Davis might not have weathered this crisis so majestically. Despite her stated preference for male assistants, Davis soon warmed to Sermak, whose retiring, ingenuous manner Davis found so soothing that, once back in Los Angeles, she invited her new employee to move in with her. The attractive young woman catered brilliantly to Davis's flammable blend of insecurity and self-importance, showing great ingenuity in the subservient flourishes that she performed for her boss: donning a chauffeur's uniform, insistently addressing her boss as 'Miss D', and bowing before company. If these gestures unsettled Davis's few remaining friends, 'Miss D' for one appreciated the filial respect so lacking in her 'real' children's behaviour toward her, and Sermak continued to play BD's stand-in until Davis's death nearly a decade later.

In 1980, Davis underwent several excruciating face-lifts, which she believed essential to keep her career alive. It seemed, however, that – only two and a half years after the AFI tribute – she had slipped once again from the public notice. For her only noteworthy role in *Family Reunion*, Davis prevailed over his mother's better judgment and recruited BD's son Ashley for a small role in the television mini-series. BD, by her own account, was right to dread Ashley's acting debut, for over the three-month shoot, Davis traumatised her 11-year-old grandson, whom she called a *rough customer*.[270] She ordered Ashley around, controlled his food intake, called his father a *pile of crap* – behaved, in short, with all the violent irrationality that BD had come to expect from Davis.[271] As BD eloquently reported it, when Ashley came back from the shoot, he told her, 'I don't know how you survived [16 years with Davis], Mom. She's nuts, stark-raving loony-toons!'[272]

Over the next few years, though she had a few more decent parts – including one as Alice Vanderbilt in the TV movie *Little Gloria . . . Happy at Last* and another as a terminally ill wife in *Right of Way*, a 1983 made-for-cable feature co-starring James Stewart – Davis still faced grave financial difficulties. Her situation had improved only slightly in the last decade, when, in 1973, she had reported her income as $26,000, a pathetic sum that comprised all royalties from her old work. (Projecting no bigger salary in 1974, the former highest-paid woman in America applied for social security benefits.) Despite her dramatically reduced income, when Jeremy Hyman's hay-hauling business, which had evolved into an interstate trucking company, went bankrupt in 1983, Davis managed to raise enough money to prevent the bank from foreclosing on her daughter's home.

The same year that Davis struggled to make the Hymans' mortgage payments, she saw a permanent end to her near-destitution when producer Aaron Spelling offered her the pulse-stopping fee of $100,000 per episode to appear on his new TV drama, *Hotel*. Each paycheque required only a single day's work, but from the first hour Davis regretted her commitment to the show. Judging the series tawdry and beneath her abilities – and her role in it hideously meagre – Davis schemed for ways to break her contract. BD admonished Davis for even contemplating leaving such a lucrative job, particularly after so many years of accepting fast-food-employee fees to play Medusa mothers in straight-to-video B-movies.

Two episodes into the series, Davis had an unexpectedly unpleasant reason for leaving *Hotel* when she noticed a large lump on her breast. Diagnosed with breast cancer – the same disease that had killed her sister Bobby only three years earlier – Davis checked into hospital, where doctors performed a radical mastectomy to remove the tumour. The operation appeared successful until nine days into Davis's recovery, when the actress suffered a mild stroke. *I was furious*, Davis said. *I did not think I deserved it. Of all the human afflictions, a stroke is about the worst*, she went on, even in her illness committed to overstatement: *I wouldn't wish it on Adolf Hitler!*[274] In her hospital bed, the actress contemplated her prospects: *Over and over, lying there, I asked, will I ever be able to work again? Acting had been my life. I wouldn't want to live if I could never act again.*[275] As these tormenting doubts mounted, Sermak never left Davis's side; BD, on the other hand, didn't visit her mother until three weeks after the surgery.

By 1984, as Davis worked full-time to recover from her stroke – it took her three months to re-learn how to use a knife and fork – BD was contending with some serious ailments of her own,

The attention that Davis received in those years was neither profitable nor particularly pleasurable. In 1981, singer Kim Carnes won a Grammy for the pop song, 'Bette Davis Eyes.' *My grandson has finally sat up and taken notice of me,* Davis said. *He loves the song and goes around saying he now knows how famous Grandma is!* But however flattering in the beginning, 'Bette Davis Eyes' soon annoyed Davis, as it represented modern audiences' primary (and perhaps only) association with her name.[273]

'They don't make films these days, they make travelogues' she said of her experience making *Death on the Nile*. 1978

including bone spurs, colitis, varicose veins, and obesity. Even after Davis had bailed them out the previous year, the Hymans' financial problems persisted, and BD derived her chief income from selling Christmas wreaths to local shops. Then, one day, while watching televangelist Pat Robertson's programme, *The 700 Club*, BD leaned forward to touch the TV screen and, just like that, her chronic back pain vanished for ever. To give thanks BD proclaimed herself a born-again Christian and, not long after this Damascene episode, she rushed to a famed Pentecostal healer in Ohio, who just as miraculously cured Ashley Hyman's partial deafness. After this shaman advised her to purge all loved ones impeding her spiritual growth from her life, BD began ringing her mother every Sunday afternoon, imploring Davis to renounce Satan and accept Christ as her personal saviour. Davis, however, wanted none of salvation, and when BD presented her mother with a leather-bound copy of *The Living Bible*, Davis burst into cruel laughter and, as BD remembered, 'used Christ as a profanity'.[276]

BD decided then and there to break free of Davis's taint. She chose a path to righteousness that promised to relieve her spiritual and financial burdens simultaneously when she accepted a publisher's advance of $100,000 to write a book about growing up with Bette Davis. It took BD a year to produce her scandalous, tell-all memoir, *My Mother's Keeper*, described on the cover as 'a daughter's candid portrait of her famous mother'.

Because BD had not considered it fit to warn her mother of her literary debut, Harold Schiff, Davis's lawyer and intimate friend, took the task on himself, ringing her up a week before the release of the book; he later said that 'it was worse than telling her that BD had died.'[277] Davis had only recently left Los Angeles for England, where she was filming *Murder with Mirrors* with Helen Hayes. Already fragile and cantankerous to be working under such stressful conditions – the Agatha Christie adaptation was her first appearance on camera since her stroke – Davis lost what little self-control she had left when *My Mother's Keeper* hit the bookstores. In 1977, Davis had relished *Mommie Dearest,* Christina Crawford's remorseless send-up of her mother Joan's insanity. *The book makes her a monster, but one gets the feeling Christina couldn't have made it up, could she?*[278] Davis asked a reporter from the *New York Times*, going on to say that: *One area of life Joan should never have gone into was* children.[279] Davis had bragged to countless interviewers that *My daughter will never be able to write a Mommie Dearest book about me*![280]

But when it was released, perversely, on Mother's Day of 1985, *My Mother's Keeper* seemed to be exactly that, an angry daughter's exhausting compendium of insults and accusations, allegations that Davis had been an 'abusive, domineering and hateful mother' and a 'grotesque alcoholic'.[281] The difference was that the abuses that Christina Crawford reported were headline-, even jail-worthy and a shocking contrast to Joan's syrupy public persona. BD's account, on the other hand, in portraying Davis as an abrasive, outspoken and terribly lonesome egomaniac accustomed to getting her way all the time – not unlike most movie stars in this respect – contained no such startling revelations. Everyone who had ever worked with Davis had contended with her massive ego and volatile temper. Of the physical therapist – 'a charming lady who was endlessly patient with Mother' – who worked with Davis after her stroke, BD reported a typical exchange: 'Mother screamed profanities. "Don't touch me, you bitch! . . . Jesus! I'll kill you if you touch me again! . . . You fucking idiot! . . . None of you are worth a shit in this place! . . . Get your hands off me! . . . You don't know what you're doing! . . . Keep your filthy hands to yourself! . . . Get the fuck out and leave me alone! . . . Shit! . . . Christ! . . . Jesus! . . . Fuck!"'[282] And so it went for almost 350 turgid pages.

Like *Mommie Dearest*, *My Mother's Keeper* generated a good deal of horror, but this time it was directed not at the memoir's subject, but at its author. Without accusing her of outright dishonesty, family friends criticised BD

Even Gary Merrill, by then 70 years old and living in a small town in Maine, picketed his local bookshop with a sign reading 'Please Boycott *My Mother's Keeper*'. Three years later, however, Merrill became a 'familial mudslinger' himself when he published his own extremely unflattering account of Davis in his memoir, *Bette, Rita, and the Rest of My Life*.[283]

– far too clumsy a writer to convey any nuance – for capturing Davis's hysteria out of context, in the least flattering light. Even those who judged BD's recollections truthful and accurate objected to her merciless timing, right on the tail of Davis's lengthy medical travails – at least Christina Crawford had waited for her mother to die before renouncing her childhood. Insisting that posthumous publication would have defeated her original goal – that of spiritual reckoning, both her and her mother's – BD denied all likenesses to Crawford's memoir, as well as any profit-mongering or insensitivity.

No one, least of all Bette Davis, cared to hear BD's self-defence. After a single terse phone conversation, Davis declared that she had no daughter, and soon afterwards the

Bored and dissatisfied on the set of the TV drama *Hotel*

Hymans absconded to the Bahamas, both to spare BD public ridicule and to shelter her husband from the massive business debts he had left unpaid in Pennsylvania. With the more than $1million she earned in royalties, BD retired into a quiet life as a horse portraitist and set about writing her next book, *Narrow Is the Way*, a detailed account of her relationship with Christ that one critic joked should be retitled *Narrow Is the Mind*. She never saw her mother again.

THE GREATEST SADIST MOVIES EVER HAD

'That book killed Bette,' one of BD's closest friends said of *My Mother's Keeper*. 'That was absolutely the end.'[284] Though Davis admitted as much herself, calling the book *as catastrophic as the stroke,* she lived for almost four years after BD's betrayal. One of her favourite lines – *Tell them I'm not above anything, except retirement* – held true until the end.[285]

Most of Davis's friends had expected the actress to blow up at her daughter, and – to infer from the frequent nonsensical rages detailed in her memoir – so did BD. Indeed, fear of that eventuality seemed in retrospect one of the Hymans' chief reasons for fleeing to the Bahamas. But instead of waging war against her daughter, Battlin' Bette, stunned, simply shut down. For the first time in her life, she was too heartbroken even to pick a fight.

In 1987, two years after the devastating release of *My Mother's Keeper*, Davis published *This 'n' That*, a scattered sort-of-sequel to her 1961 autobiography, *The Lonely Life*. Readers anticipating a blow-by-blow response to BD were disappointed, for Davis only mentioned her daughter in the book's epilogue, in the uncharacteristically crisp form of a letter addressed to 'Hyman'. *There is no doubt that you have great potential as a writer of fiction. You have always been a great storyteller,* Davis coolly addressed her daughter. *The sum total of your having written this book is a glaring lack of loyalty and thanks for the very privileged life I feel you have been given.* Then, in the postscript: *I hope someday I will understand the title* My Mother's Keeper. *If it refers to money, if my memory serves me right, I've been your keeper all these many years. I am continuing to do so, as my name has made your book about me a success.* [286]

And that was all. BD's memoir may well have destroyed Davis, but she never brought it up again – in public, at least, her indomitable 'Yankee Dame' attitude triumphed over her personal sorrows. Davis became, in those years, something of a living national monument, a staple of the late-night talk-show circuit as 'a fabulous no-flies-on-me Yankee "personality"', the recipient of innumerable awards. [287] She declined no invitation – particularly not those involving flashbulbs and raucous encores – and in the last 18 months of her life Davis travelled tens of thousands of miles to accept the sundry honours flung at her. In all these public appearances, Davis – though her weight had dropped first to 88, then to a skeletal 75 pounds – faltered on only a few occasions, most notably during the 1987 Academy Awards telecast, when she presented the Best Actor trophy to Paul Newman without first reading out the nominees. Before an audience of several billion, Davis came across as muddled, semi-senile, but she recovered her acerbic wit swiftly, and within the hour she was blaming the embarrassment on shuffled cue cards and the ceremony's incompetent director.

While Davis flitted from one lifetime achievement ceremony to the next, accepting plaques and making speeches, she only seldom acted, prompting one director to observe that 'Many give Bette Davis dinners but very few give her jobs.'[288] Ever-hungry, right up to the end, for just one more big break, Davis never stopped playing the part of the star: she dressed formally for every appearance – even at her local grocery store.

To rationalise her reputation for never refusing a role, Davis always mentioned her financial problems in conjunction with her bottomless need for public attention: *Some people can never get it into their stupid, stupid heads that a star can work for 50 years and still not have any decent money put away. Certainly I don't! So I slave and slave and grub and grub and take a lot of perfectly awful stuff for the money – and yes, for the continued exposure.*[289] However mercenary her motives, on the rare occasion that she did receive a decent part, Davis lapsed into her same old mannerisms, justifying one critic's opinion that she had more guts than taste: 'She felt secure only in roles she could Bettify.'[290]

But after her stroke robbed her of her greatest strengths as an actress – her easy manipulation of her body and gift for physical exaggeration – Davis began to find even self-imitation a challenge. In 1987, when she made *The Whales of August* with fellow Golden Age veteran Lillian Gish, only bitterness survived in her performance. Though Davis was 78 to Gish's 90, her medical trials had so ravaged her appearance that she, not Gish, played the elder woman in this quiet picture about two ageing sisters on the

Davis together with Lillian Gish in *The Whales of August,* a final and bitter swansong 1987

coast of Maine. Electricity between the actresses never sparked, principally because Davis regarded Gish – who had achieved fame in DW Griffith's *Birth of a Nation* in 1915, when Davis was only seven – as a tremendous threat. Even after the mild-mannered Gish readily surrendered top billing to her co-star, Davis carped over every production detail, opposed even the gentlest overtures from the crew, and – because it fell on Gish's birthday – refused to attend the film's New York premiere. Mired in unreciprocated hostility, Davis was so busy hating Gish that she forgot altogether to act.

By then the frail actress was in constant pain, shrinking daily and living on tranquilisers. In the summer of 1989, her cancer returned, forcing Davis to undergo a series of debilitating radiation treatments. Though her rapid deterioration was evident in all television appearances and magazine photos – dramatic enough to prompt BD to call her mother once more – Davis never admitted that she was terminally ill, claiming instead that she had just lost her appetite temporarily. In September 1989, Davis shrugged off the advice of her doctors when she elected to travel 8,000 miles to accept another lifetime-achievement award at a film festival in San Sebastian, Spain. Sermak – described by one acquaintance as a 'real "Eve Harrington" employee' and by BD as the 'willing victim' her mother still required – kept close watch over 'Miss D' for the duration of the festival.[291] But on 3 October, Davis lost all strength. She was flown to a hospital in Paris, where she died three days later, on 6 October 1989. A week later, after a crowded memorial service – at which only BD was notably absent – Davis was buried between Ruthie and Bobby on a hill overlooking the Warner Brothers studios, beneath a tombstone that read, 'Bette Davis: She did it the hard way.'

Davis's will was not made public until six weeks afterwards. In a carefully worded ten-page document dated 2 September 1987, Davis divided her estate, which was valued between $600,000 and $1 million (a day's pay for a major contemporary movie star), between her son, Michael, and her personal assistant, Kathryn Sermak: 'I declare that I have intentionally and with full knowledge omitted to provide herein for my daughter, Margot, and my daughter, Barbara, and-or my grandsons, Ashley Hyman and Justin Hyman.'[292] 'Unfortunately, the mother (Hyman) had her children follow her rather than their hearts,' Harold Schiff, the executor of Davis's estate, said of the exclusion of Davis's grandchildren. 'Down the road they'll be sorry. Twenty years from now, they'll say, "That was my grandmother and why didn't we know her?"'[293]

Who is Bette Davis? Davis once tried to determine. *An actress from New England. A good actress. One whom people have learned to love.*[294] But perhaps she gave a better reply to another reporter who asked her to condense her character into five words or less: *I'm just too much,* she answered with no hesitation.[295]

Notes

1 Bette Davis with Sanford Dody, *The Lonely Life* (New York: 1961) p 11.

2 Lawrence Quirk, *Fasten Your Seatbelts: The Passionate Life of Bette Davis* (New York: 1991) p 16.

3 James Spada, *More Than a Woman* (New York: 1993) p 10.

4 Davis, *The Lonely Life*, p 12.

5 Davis, *The Lonely Life*, p 12.

6 Barbara Leaming, *Bette Davis* (London: 1992) p 37.

7 Boze Hadleigh, *Bette Davis Speaks* (New York: 1996) p 200.

8 Davis, *The Lonely Life*, p 22.

9 Davis, *The Lonely Life*, p 28.

10 Davis, *The Lonely Life*, p 23.

11 Davis, *The Lonely Life*, p 23.

12 Davis, *The Lonely Life*, p 25.

13 Spada, *More Than a Woman*, p 27.

14 *People* magazine, 21 March 1977.

15 Leaming, *Bette Davis*, p 21.

16 Spada, *More Than a Woman*, p 33.

17 Leaming, *Bette Davis*, p 35.

18 Davis, *The Lonely Life*, p 39.

19 Davis, *The Lonely Life*, p 39.

20 Leaming, *Bette Davis*, p 37.

21 Whitney Stine, *I'd Love to Kiss You* (New York: 1990) p 201.

22 Quirk, *Fasten Your Seatbelts*, p 92.

23 Spada, *More Than a Woman*, p 55.

24 Leaming, *Bette Davis*, p 41.

25 Spada, *More Than a Woman*, p 55.

26 Davis, *The Lonely Life*, p 50.

27 Davis, *The Lonely Life*, p 51.

28 Davis, *The Lonely Life*, p 48.

29 Hadleigh, *Bette Davis Speaks*, p 107.

30 Davis, *The Lonely Life*, p 56.

31 Davis, *The Lonely Life*, p 68.

32 Davis, *The Lonely Life*, 72.

33 Hadleigh, *Bette Davis Speaks*, 76.

34 Spada, *More Than a Woman*, p 84.

35 Hadleigh, *Bette Davis Speaks*, p 58.

36 Davis, *The Lonely Life*, p 60.

37 Emmanuel Levy, *George Cukor, Master of Elegance: Hollywood's Legendary Director and His Stars* (New York: 1994) p 37.

38 Spada, *More Than a Woman*, p 69.

39 Stine, *I'd Love to Kiss You*, p 67.

40 Davis, *The Lonely Life*, p 80.

41 Quirk, *Fasten Your Seatbelts*, p 26.

42 Davis, *The Lonely Life*, p 87.

43 http://www.duke.edu/~azf2/quotes.html

44 Hadleigh, *Bette Davis Speaks*, p 142.

45 http://xroads.virginia.edu/~UG02/FILM/printdepression.html

46 Andrew Bergman, *We're in the Money: Depression America and its Film* (New York: 1971) p 92.

47 Spada, *More Than a Woman*, p 70.

48 Stine, *I'd Love to Kiss You*, p 166.

49 Shaun Considine, *Bette and Joan: The Divine Feud* (London: 1989) p 117.

50 Spada, *More Than a Woman*, p 72.

51 Rush in *Weekly Variety*, quoted in Gene Ringgold, *The Films of Bette Davis* (New Jersey: 1966) p 25.

52 Leaming, *Bette Davis*, p 79.

53 John Baxter, *Hollywood in the Thirties* (London: 1968).

54 Philip French, *The Movie Moguls: An Informal History of the Hollywood Tycoons* (London: 1969) p 47.

55 Pauline Kael, *5000 Nights at the Movies* (New York: 1982) p 238.

56 Davis, *The Lonely Life*, p 136; *Bette Davis: A Basically Benevolent Volcano* (TV documentary, 1983)

57 Regina Crewe in the *New York American*; quoted in Ringgold, *Films of Bette Davis*, p 32.

58 *Bette Davis: A Basically Benevolent Volcano* (TV documentary, 1983).

59 Davis, *The Lonely Life*, p 134.

60 Stine, *I'd Love to Kiss You*, p 35.

61 Spada, *More Than a Woman*, 126.

62 *The Dick Cavett Show*, 1971. Quoted in Whitney Stine, *Mother Goddam: the Story of the Career of Bette Davis* (New York: 1974) p 3.

63 Davis, *The Lonely Life*, p 101.

64 Hadleigh, Bette Davis Speaks, p 60.

65 David Thomson, *The New Biographical Dictionary of Film* (New York: 2002) p 208.

66 Quirk, *Fasten Your Seatbelts*, p 113.

67 Ringgold, *Films of Bette Davis*, p 57.

68 Quirk, *Fasten Your Seatbelts*, p 109.

69 Quirk, *Fasten Your Seatbelts*, p 109.

70 Davis, *The Lonely Life*, p 147.

71 Stine, *I'd Love to Kiss You*, 127.

72 *Film Weekly*, 29 March 1935.

73 Quirk, *Fasten Your Seatbelts*, p 113.

74 Leaming, *Bette Davis*, p 93.

75 Hadleigh, *Bette Davis Speaks*, p 18.

76 Leaming, *Bette Davis*, p 139.

77 The Kennedy Center Honors: A Celebration of the Performing Arts (TV), March 1987.

78 Hadleigh, *Bette Davis Speaks*, p 144.

79 'Stardom or Serfdom?' American Studies Department of the University of Virginia, see http://xroads.virginia.edu/~UG02/FILM/starserfdom.html

80 Stine, *I'd Love to Kiss You*, p 19.

81 Considine, *Bette and Joan*, p 136.

82 Davis, *The Lonely Life*, p 150.

83 Stine, *I'd Love to Kiss You*, p 150.

84 Hadleigh, *Bette Davis Speaks*, p 57.

85 Spada, *More Than a Woman*, p 205.

86 Spada, *More Than a Woman*, p 176.

87 Spada, *More Than a Woman*, p 178.

88 Leaming, *Bette Davis*, p 104.

89 Leaming, *Bette Davis*, p 106.

90 Leaming, *Bette Davis*, p 108.

91 *Bette Davis: A Basically Benevolent Volcano* (TV documentary, 1983).

92 Leaming, *Bette Davis*, p 108.

93 Hadleigh, Bette Davis Speaks, p 115.

94 Davis, *The Lonely Life*, p 174.

95 *Bette Davis: A Basically Benevolent Volcano* (TV documentary, 1983).

96 Davis, *The Lonely Life*, p 185.

97 Tom Flannery, *1939 The Year in Movies* (Jefferson, North Carolina: 1990) p 41.

98 Thomson, *Biographical Dictionary*, p 208.

99 Frank Nugent in *The New York Times*; quoted in Ringgold, *Films of Bette Davis*, p 92.

100 Ringgold, *Films of Bette Davis*, p 95.

101 Kael, *5000 Nights*, p 384.

102 'All About Bette,' by Jim Bawden in *The Toronto Star*, 9 October 1989.

103 Stine, *I'd Love to Kiss You*, p 57.

104 Frank Nugent in *The New York Times*; quoted in Ringgold, *Films of Bette Davis*, p 100.

105 Spada, *More Than a Woman*, p 230.

106 Kael, *5000 Nights*, p 410.

107 Leaming, *Bette Davis*, p 138.

108 Spada, *More Than a Woman*, 252.

109 For more information on World War Two and Hollywood, see Roy Hoopes, *When the Stars Went to War* (New York: 1994).

110 Spada, *More Than a Woman*, p 268.

111 Considine, *Bette and Joan*, p 131.

112 Considine, *Bette and Joan*, p 129.

113 Spada, *More Than a Woman*, p 262.

114 Stine, *I'd Love to Kiss You*, 139.

115 Stine, *I'd Love to Kiss You*, pp 140.

116 Spada, *More Than a Woman*, p 284.

117 Leaming, *Bette Davis*, p 173.

118 'Bette from Boston', *Silver Screen*, cited in Maria Laplace, 'Stars and the Star System: the Case of Bette Davis' in *The Film Studies Reader*, ed Joanne Hollows (London: 2000)

119 'Bette Davis,' *Life*, 8 January 1939.

120 'Bette Davis,' *Life*, 8 January 1939; Hadleigh, *Bette Davis Speaks*, p 150.

121 James Agee, *Agee on Film* (New York: 1958) p 80.

122 Agee, *Agee on Film*, p 43.

123 Kael, *5000 Nights at the Movies*, p 536.

124 Stine, *I'd Love to Kiss You*, p 20.

125 Charles Higham, *Bette Davis* (New York: 1981) p 169.

126 Higham, *Bette Davis*, p 136.

127 Spada, *More Than a Woman*, p 273.

128 Spada, *More Than a Woman*, p 273.

129 Davis, *The Lonely Life*, 203.

130 Hadleigh, *Bette Davis Speaks*, p 39.

131 Stine, *I'd Love to Kiss You,* p 22

132 Stine, *I'd Love to Kiss You*, p 114.

133 Leaming, *Bette Davis*, p 163.

134 http://www.anecdotage.com/index.php?aid=189

135 http://www.born-today.com/Today/d12-12.htm

136 Sam Staggs, *All About All About Eve* (New York: 2000) p 220.

137 Spada, *More Than a Woman*, p 255.

138 Spada, *More Than a Woman*, p 259.

139 Leaming, *Bette Davis*, p 169.

140 Hadleigh, *Bette Davis Speaks*, 272.

141 Quirk, *Fasten Your Seatbelts*, p 279.

142 Quirk, *Fasten Your Seatbelts*, p 279.

143 Higham, *Bette Davis*, p 250.

144 Hadleigh, *Bette Davis Speaks*, p 214.

145 Hadleigh, *Bette Davis Speaks*, p 114.

146 Spada, *More Than a Woman*, p 312.

147 Leaming, *Bette Davis*, p 177;
     Higham, *Bette Davis*, p 242.

148 Spada, *More Than a Woman*, p 315.

149 Agee, *Agee on Film*, p 80.

150 Hadleigh, *Bette Davis Speaks*, p 60.

151 Spada, *More Than a Woman*, p 101.

152 Davis, *The Lonely Life*, 134.

153 Stine, *I'd Love to Kiss You*, p 221.

154 Quirk, *Fasten Your Seatbelts*, p 416.

155 Hadleigh, *Bette Davis Speaks*,
     p 156.

156 Hadleigh, *Bette Davis Speaks*,
     p 196.

157 Hadleigh, *Bette Davis Speaks*, 156

158 Agee, *Agee on Film*, p 145.

159 *Bette Davis: A Basically Benevolent
     Volcano* (TV documentary, 1983).

160 Hadleigh, *Bette Davis Speaks*,
     p 158.

161 Stine, *Mother Goddam*, p 172

162 Spada, *More Than a Woman*, p 333.

163 Ringgold, *Films of Bette Davis*,
     p 135.

164 Spada, *More Than a Woman*, p 400.

l65 Stine, *I'd Love to Kiss You*, p 133.

166 Stine, *I'd Love to Kiss You*, p 134.

167 Leaming, *Bette Davis*, p 193.

168 Stine, *I'd Love to Kiss You*, 193.

169 'Bette, A Hollywood Silver-Screen
     Legend' by Jim Emerson in *The
     Seattle Times*, 21 February 1988.

170 Spada, *More Than a Woman*, p 358.

171 Leaming, *Bette Davis*, p 185

172 Spada, *More Than a Woman*, p 332;
     p 358

173 Leaming, *Bette Davis*, p 188.

174 Davis, *The Lonely Life*, p 221.

175 Spada, *More Than a Woman*, p 353.

176 Spada, *More Than a Woman*, p 356.

177 Spada, *More Than a Woman*, 361.

178 Spada, *More Than a Woman*, p 365.

179 Spada, *More Than a Woman*, p 370.

180 Spada, *More Than a Woman*, p 382.

181 Spada, *More Than a Woman*, p 381.

182 Davis, *The Lonely Life*, 227.

183 Spada, *More Than a Woman*, p 385.

184 Staggs, *All About All About Eve*,
     p 93.

185 'Bette Davis' by Janice Berman in
     Newsday, 23 April 1989.

186 Hadleigh, *Bette Davis Speaks*,
     p 172, 234.

187 Staggs, *All About All About Eve*,
     p 118.

188 Davis, *The Lonely Life*, p 225.

189 Spada, *More Than a Woman*, p 400.

190 Ringgold, *Films of Bette Davis*, p
     150.

191 Staggs, *All About All About Eve*,
     p 208.

192 Spada, *More Than a Woman*, p 390.

193 Davis, *The Lonely Life*, p 227.

194 Considine, *Bette and Joan*, p 243.

195 Staggs, *All About All About Eve*,
     p 112.

196 Spada, *More Than a Woman*, p 403.

197 Staggs, *All About All About Eve*,
     p 193.

198 Davis, *The Lonely Life*, p 228.

199 Stine, *I'd Love to Kiss You*, 218.

200 'Gary Merrill's Life with Bette and
     Rita' by Marian Christy in *The
     Boston Globe*, 29 January 1989.

201 Ringgold, *Films of Bette Davis*,
     p 155.

202 Leaming, *Bette Davis*, p 239.

203 Considine, *Bette and Joan*, p 264.

204 Davis, *The Lonely Life*, p 233.

205 Spada, *More Than a Woman*, p 429.

206 Davis, *The Lonely Life*, 237.

207 Davis, *The Lonely Life*, 240.

208 'Gary Merrill's Life with Bette and Rita' by Marian Christy in *The Boston Globe*, 29 January 1989.

209 Higham, 289.

210 Stine, *I'd Love to Kiss You*, p 218.

211 Considine, *Bette and Joan*, p 294.

212 Spada, *More Than a Woman*, p 447.

213 Stine, *I'd Love to Kiss You*, 75.

214 Hadleigh, *Bette Davis Speaks*, p 147.

215 Spada, *More Than a Woman*, p 452.

216 Spada, *More Than a Woman*, p 457.

217 Spada, *More Than a Woman*, p 457.

218 Davis, *The Lonely Life*, p 245.

219 Hadleigh, *Bette Davis Speaks*, p 39.

220 Hadleigh, *Bette Davis Speaks*, p 197.

221 Hadleigh, *Bette Davis Speaks*, p 197.

222 Spada, *More Than a Woman*, p 511.

223 Quirk, *Fasten Your Seatbelts*, p 385.

224 Davis, *The Lonely Life*, p 246.

225 Leaming, *Bette Davis*, p 230.

226 Spada, *More Than a Woman*, p 485.

227 Stine, *I'd Love to Kiss You*, p 124.

228 Bette Davis with Michael Hershkowitz, *This 'n' That* (New York: 1987) p 106.

229 'All About Bette,' by Jim Bawden in *The Toronto Star*, 9 October 1989.

230 Considine, *Bette and Joan*, p 95.

231 Hadleigh, *Bette Davis Speaks*, p 109.

232 Stine, *I'd Love to Kiss You*, p 45.

233 Stine, *I'd Love to Kiss You*, p 48.

234 Leaming, *Bette Davis*, p 240.

235 Spada, *More Than a Woman*, p 515.

236 Spada, *More Than a Woman*, p 515.

237 *Bette Davis: A Basically Benevolent Volcano* (TV documentary, 1983).

238 Hadleigh, *Bette Davis Speaks*, p 177.

239 Spada, *More Than a Woman*, p 516.

240 Ringgold, *Films of Bette Davis*, p 178.

241 Ringgold, *Films of Bette Davis*, p 178.

242 Spada, *More Than a Woman*, p 520.

243 'All About Bette' by Jim Bawden in *The Toronto Star*, 9 October 1989.

244 Kael, *5000 Nights*, p 346.

245 Spada, *More Than a Woman*, p 544.

246 Thomson, *Biographical Dictionary*, p 209.

247 Pauline Kael, *For Keeps* (New York: 1994) p 582.

248 Quirk, *Fasten Your Seatbelts*, p 371.

249 Spada, *More Than a Woman*, p 414.

250 Davis, *The Lonely Life*, p 144.

251 Hadleigh, *Bette Davis Speaks*, p 180.

252 Stine, *I'd Love to Kiss You*, p. 165.

253 http://womenshistory.about.com/library/qu/blqudavi.htm

254 Considine, *Bette and Joan*, p 304.

255 Staggs, *All About All About Eve*, p 241.

256 Considine, *Bette and Joan*, p 400.

257 Leaming, *Bette Davis*, p 243.

258 Spada, *More Than a Woman*, p 565.

259 Spada, *More Than a Woman*, p 566.

260 Spada, *More Than a Woman*, p 558.

261 Quirk, *Fasten Your Seatbelts*, p 416.

262 'Oft-Told Tales' by Dean Goodman in *The San Francisco Chronicle*, 8 September 1993

263 'All About Bette' by Jim Bawden in *The Toronto Star*, 9 October 1989.

264 Spada, *More Than a Woman*, p 595.

265 Spada, *More Than a Woman*, p 602.

266 Spada, *More Than a Woman*, p 602.

267 Spada, *More Than a Woman*, p 611.

268 Quirk, *Fasten Your Seatbelts*, p 420.

269 Quirk, *Fasten Your Seatbelts*, p 422.

270 B D Hyman, *My Mother's Keeper* (New York: 1985) p 261.

271 Hyman, *My Mother's Keeper*, p 255.

272 Hyman, *My Mother's Keeper*, p 272.

273 Quirk, *Fasten Your Seatbelts*, p 431.

274 Considine, *Bette and Joan*, p 433.

275 Spada, *More Than a Woman*, p 619.

276 Spada, *More Than a Woman*, p 634.

277 Spada, *More Than a Woman*, p 638.

278 Considine, *Bette and Joan*, p 433.

279 Considine, *Bette and Joan*, p 433.

280 'All About Bette' by Jim Bawden in *The Toronto Star*, 9 October 1989.

281 'Bette Davis Estate Near $1 Million,' *Los Angeles Times*, 7 November 1989

282 Hyman, *My Mother's Keeper*, p 334.

283 Davis, *This 'n' That*, p 174.

284 Spada, *More Than a Woman*, p 634.

285 'Bette Davis Dies of Cancer in Paris' by Jane Southward in *Sun Herald*, 8 October 1989.

286 Davis, *This 'n' That*, pp 169-170.

287 'The Davis Legend Anew' by Liz Smith in *Newsday*, 19 May 1992.

288 Leaming, *Bette Davis*, p 442.

289 Spada, *More Than a Woman*, 647.

290 'Hurricane Bette' by David Elliot in *The Los Angeles Times*, 17 May 1992.

291 Spada, *More Than a Woman*, pp 668, 673.

292 'They Didn't Get Bette Davis Ayes', *The Associated Press*, 7 November 1989.

293 'Davis' Will Snubs Daughter', *The San Francisco Chronicle*, 7 November 1989.

294 Hadleigh, *Bette Davis Speaks*, p 274.

295 'Being Bette Davis: It's All in the Swivel' by Jim Koch in *The New York Times*, 24 March 1987.

Chronology

Year	Age	Life
1907		1 July: Harlow Morrell Davis marries Ruth Favor.
1908		5 April: Ruth Elizabeth Davis born in Lowell, Massachusetts.
1909	1	25 October: Barbara 'Bobby' Harriet Davis born.
1911	3	Ruthie Davis checks into sanatorium suffering from exhaustion and depression.
1915	7	Harlow and Ruthie Davis separate for the first time.
1918	10	Harlow and Ruth Davis divorce.
1919	11	Betty and Bobby Davis sent to boarding school while Ruthie works as governess to support them. Betty Davis burned at Christmas party.
1921	13	Ruthie Davis moves her daughters to Harlem so that she can complete a course in portrait photography. Betty Davis changes the spelling of her name.
1922	14	The Davis family moves to New Jersey, where Ruthie works as photo developer. When Bette Davis becomes depressed and Ruthie comes down with osteomyelitis of the jaw, the family returns to Massachusetts.
1923	15	Davis begins Newton High School.
1924	16	Ruthie moves her daughters to a small parochial school, where both Bette and Bobby are miserable.

Year	History	Culture
1907	Anglo-Russian Entente. Electric washing-machine invented.	Daily attendance at nickelodeons exceeds 2 million.
1908	Austria-Hungary annexes Bosnia-Herzegovina.	E M Forster, *A Room with a View.* Cubism begins.
1909	Henry Ford introduces Model T car.	F T Marinetto publishes manifesto of futurism in *Le Figaro.*
1911	Amundsen reaches South Pole. Ernest Rutherford discovers the nuclear model of the atom.	Puccini, *The Girl of the Golden West* (opera). Stravinsky, *The Firebird* (ballet). E M Forster, *Howard's End*
1915	Dardanelles/Gallipoli campaign (until 1916).	Twelve-reel *Birth of a Nation,* first modern motion picture, grosses $18m. Picasso, *Harlequin.*
1918	In Russia, Tsar Nicholas II and family executed. 11 November: Armistice agreement ends First World War.	Amédée Ozenfant and Le Corbusier, *Après le Cubisme.* Paul Klee, *Gartenplan. Tarzan of the Apes* with Elmo Lincoln.
1919	In US, prohibition begins. Irish Civil War (until 1921).	Charlie Chaplin, Douglas Fairbanks, D W Griffith and Mary Pickford form United Artists.
1921	Allies fixes Germany's reparation payments: Rhineland occupied.	Sergey Prokofiev, *The Love of Three Oranges.* Chaplin, *The Kid.*
1922	Soviet Union formed. Benito Mussolini's fascists march on Rome.	Will Hays is appointed head of the new MPPDA, which has a censorship division that becomes known as the 'Hays Office'.
1923	End of the Ottoman empire ends.	Le Corbusier, *Vers une architecture.*
1924	Vladimir Lenin dies.	Forster, *A Passage to India.* Thomas Mann, *The Magic Mountain.* André Breton, first surrealist manifesto.

Year	Age	Life
1925	17	Davis transfers to Cushing Academy. In Peterborough, New Hampshire, that summer, Davis performs before a paying audience for the first time as Moth in *A Midsummer Night's Dream*.
1926	18	Bette Davis graduates from Cushing Academy. She spends the next year depressed, contemplating the future.
1927	19	After the happiest summer of her life on Cape Cod, where she worked as a lifeguard, Bette Davis is rejected by the Eva LaGallienne Civic Repertory Company; a month later, she begins training at the Anderson School of the Theatre in Manhattan.
1928	20	Summer: Davis is fired from George Cukor's repertory company in Rochester. Fall: Davis makes her off-Broadway debut in *The Earth Between*, then goes on a national tour as Hedvig in *The Wild Duck*.
1929	21	Davis makes her Broadway debut in *Broken Dishes;* fails screen test for Samuel Goldwyn.
1930	22	Davis appears in her second Broadway production, the short-lived *Solid South*; signs her first contract with Universal, and after a five-day train journey, arrives in Los Angeles for the first time late that December.
1931	23	Davis makes film debut in *Bad Sister*. Appears in 6 more films until Universal declines to renew her contract. Appears in *The Man Who Played God* with George Arliss at Warner Brothers. Dyes her hair platinum and decides to go glamorous.
1932	24	Bobby suffers severe nervous breakdown. January: Davis signs 7-year contract with Warner Brothers. 18 August: Marries Harmon Oscar Nelson, a jazz musician she met at Cushing Academy. First notable onscreen performance in *Cabin in the Cotton*. Another pleasant but forgettable appearance in *Three on a Match*.
1933	25	Davis's first abortion. Sees her name above the title for the first time in *Ex-Lady*, but Davis is unhappy with the trashy roles Warners is dishing out.
1934	26	Stars opposite Leslie Howard as Mildred in *Of Human Bondage* at RKO. Other pictures that year include *Fashions of 1934* and *Housewife*.
1935	27	Davis plays a satisfying supporting role in *Bordertown* opposite Paul Muni. Also stars in *The Girl from Tenth Avenue* and *Dangerous*. After these promising roles, Davis is unhappy with her next two assignments, *Front Page Woman* and *Special Agent*.

Year	History	Culture
1925	Chiang Kai-shek launches campaign to unify China. Discovery of ionosphere.	F Scott Fitzgerald, *The Great Gatsby*. Kafka, *The Trial*
1926	Hirohito becomes emperor of Japan.	A A Milne, *Winnie the Pooh*. Fritz Lang, *Metropolis*
1927	Joseph Stalin comes to power. Charles Lindbergh flies across Atlantic.	Warner Brothers releases *The Jazz Singer*, the first of the 'talkies'.
1928	Kellogg-Briand Pact for Peace. Alexander Fleming discovers penicillin.	Mickey Mouse makes his debut in the short cartoon, 'Steamboat Willie'.
1929	Wall Street crash. Young Plan for Germany.	First Academy Awards are announced.
1930	Mahatma Gandhi leads Salt March in India. Frank Whittle patents turbo-jet engine. Pluto discovered.	The Hays Office institutes the Production Code guidelines of moral standards in the movies.
1931	King Alfonso XIII flees; Spanish republic formed. Building of Empire State Building completed in New York.	Rakhmaninov's music banned in the USSR as 'decadent'. St-Exupéry, *Vol de nuit*. *City Lights* (starring Charlie Chaplin)
1932	Kingdom of Saudi Arabia independent. Kingdom of Iraq independent. James Chadwick discovers neutron. First autobahn opened, between Cologne and Bonn.	Aldous Huxley, *Brave New World*. Jules Romains, *Les homes de bonne volonté*. Bertolt Brecht, *The Mother*. Thomas Beecham founds London Philharmonic Orchestra.
1933	Adolf Hitler appointed German chancellor. F D Roosevelt president in US; launches New Deal.	André Malraux, *La condition humaine*. Gertrude Stein, *The Autobiography of Alice B Toklas*
1934	In China, Mao Tse Tung starts on the Long March.	Agatha Christie, *Murder on the Orient Express*. Henry Miller, *Tropic of Cancer*
1935	In Germany, Nuremberg Laws enacted. Philippines becomes self-governing. Italy invades Ethiopia.	George Gershwin, *Porgy and Bess*. Marx Brothers, *A Night at the Opera*

Year	Age	Life
1936	28	February: Davis receives first Academy Award for *Dangerous*. Has small, agreeable role in *The Petrified Forest*, then larger roles in abominable films, *The Golden Arrow* and *Satan Met a Lady*. June: Davis flees to England to contest her contract and work for Ludovico Toeplitz. Jack Warner takes her to court; Davis loses the case and incurs massive debts.
1937	29	Davis returns to Warners to star in several high-grossing – and high-quality – pictures (*Marked Woman, Kid Galahad*, *That Certain Woman*, and *It's Love I'm After*). Bette Davis works with director William Wyler on *Jezebel*. Star and director conduct a passionate affair.
1938	30	New Year's Day: Harlow Morrell Davis dies of a heart attack. Harmon Nelson divorces Bette Davis. Davis stars in *The Sisters* with Errol Flynn. *Jezebel* released to tremendous acclaim; Davis appears on the cover of *Time* magazine.
1939	31	February: Davis wins her second Academy Award for *Jezebel*. Stars in four blockbusters (*Dark Victory, Juarez, The Old Maid*, and *The Private Lives of Elizabeth and Essex*). Retreats to New England to recover from exhaustion. Nominated for a 1940 Academy Award for her performance in *Dark Victory*. *Gone With the Wind* becomes the first major motion picture produced independently.
1940	32	Davis makes her second picture with William Wyler, *The Letter*, for which she receives an Academy Award nomination. Davis makes *All This and Heaven, Too*, her highest-grossing picture yet. 30 December: Marries for a second time, to Arthur Farnsworth.
1941	33	Davis makes lacklustre comedy with James Cagney, *The Bride Came C O D*. Stars in *The Great Lie* and *The Little Foxes,* the latter of which earns her an Academy Award nomination. End of professional relationship with William Wyler. October: Becomes first female president of the Motion Picture Academy of Arts and Sciences, a position she resigns only six weeks later. Takes supporting role in *The Man Who Came to Dinner*.
1942	34	Davis nominated for Academy Award for *Now, Voyager*. Stars in *In This Our Life*. 3 October: Hollywood Canteen opens amid much fanfare with Davis at the helm. Becomes the highest-paid woman in America.
1943	35	Davis makes two patriotic pictures, *Watch on the Rhine* and *Thank Your Lucky Stars*, in addition to *Old Acquaintance*. 23 August: Arthur Farnsworth collapses on Hollywood Boulevard, and dies without regaining consciousness.

Year	History	Culture
1936	Germany occupies Rhineland. Edward VIII abdicates throne in Britain; George VI becomes king. Spanish Civil War (until 1939).	First American motion-picture documentary. RCA experiments with television broadcasts from the Empire State Building.
1937	Japan invades China: Nanjing massacre. Arab-Jewish conflict in Palestine.	Jean-Paul Sartre, *La Nausée*. John Steinbeck, *Of Mice and Men*. Picasso, *Guernica*
1938	Kristallnacht: in Germany, Jewish houses, synagogues and schools are burnt down, and shops looted.	Warner Brothers produce *Confessions of a Nazi Spy*, although Germany represents 30% of the profits.
1939	1 September: Germany invades Poland. Francisco Franco becomes dictator of Spain. Britain and France declare war on Germany.	Steinbeck, *The Grapes of Wrath*. John Ford, *Stagecoach* (starring John Wayne). David O Selznick, *Gone with the Wind* (starring Vivien Leigh and Clark Gable)
1940	Germany occupies France, Belgium, the Netherlands, Norway and Denmark. In Britain, Winston Churchill becomes PM.	Graham Greene, *The Power and the Glory*. Ernest Hemingway, *For Whom the Bell Tolls*. Chaplin, *The Great Dictator*. Disney, *Fantasia*.
1941	Germany invades Soviet Union. In US, Lend-Lease Bill passed. Atlantic Charter signed. Japan attacks Pearl Harbour: US enter Second World War. In US, Manhattan Project begins.	First commercial television station begins broadcasting. Fitzgerald's Hollywood novel, *The Last Tycoon*, is published posthumously.
1942	German Sixth Army encircled in Stalingrad; Erwin Rommel defeated at El Alamein.	Frank Sinatra makes stage debut in New York. *Casablanca* (starring Ingrid Bergman and Humphrey Bogart)
1943	Allies bomb Germany. Allies invade Italy: Mussolini deposed. Albert Hoffman discovers hallucinogenic properties of LSD.	Rodgers and Hammerstein, *Oklahoma*. Sartre, *Being and Nothingness*. T S Eliot, *Four Quartets*

Year	Age	Life
1944	36	Bette Davis receives Academy Award nomination for *Mr Skeffington.* Stars in fund-raising picture, *Hollywood Canteen.* Conducts affair with Corporal Lewis Riley, a serviceman she met at the Canteen.
1945	37	Davis unsuccessfully courts Corporal Lewis Riley, whom she met at the Hollywood Canteen, near his training base in Georgia. Stars in *The Corn Is Green.* 27 November: Gets married for the third time to William Grant Sherry. For the first time in six years, Davis receives no Academy Award nomination.
1946	38	Davis establishes her own production company, BD Inc, and releases independent picture, *A Stolen Life*, in which she plays twins. The film earns a great deal of money, but again Davis receives no Oscar nomination. The Davis vehicle, *Deception*, loses money at the box office.
1947	39	After dissolving BD Inc, Davis requests leave of absence and on May 1 gives birth by Caesarean section to Barbara Davis Sherry.
1948	40	Stars in *Winter Meeting*, which loses almost 1.5m at the box office. Stars in dim comedy, *June Bride*, which does little to restore her reputation.
1949	41	Davis stars in the universally panned *Beyond the Forest.* After 18 years, Davis is released from her contract at Warner Bros.
1950	42	Twentieth Century Fox Head Darryl Zanuck hires Davis to replace Claudette Colbert as the star of *All About Eve.* Davis's third marriage ends in divorce. Meets and marries Gary Merrill, her fourth and last husband.
1951	43	Davis receives much praise for her role in *Payment on Demand.*
1952	44	Davis trails husband to England to co-star in *Another Man's Poison*; later that year does the same in the Merrill vehicle, *Phone Call from a Stranger.* Receives an Oscar nomination for *The Star.* Moves to New York City to star in her first stage production in over two decades, Ogden Nash's *Two's Company.* Becomes addicted to amphetamines during the production.
1953	45	Davis has half her jaw removed in an operation; buys farmhouse and moves her family to Maine. Spends next several years playing house-wife and supermom.

Year	History	Culture
1944	Allies land in Normandy: Paris is liberated. Civil war in Greece.	*Lay My Burden Down* (documentary about former slaves). Adorno and Horkheimer's essay on the 'Culture Industry'
1945	8 May: Germany surrenders. United Nations formed. F D Roosevelt dies; Harry Truman becomes US president. Atomic bombs dropped on Hiroshima and Nagasaki.	Benjamin Britten, *Peter Grimes*. George Orwell, *Animal Farm*. Karl Popper, *The Open Society and Its Enemies*. UNESCO founded.
1946	In Argentina, Juan Perón becomes president. In Britain, National Health Service founded. Winston Churchill makes 'Iron Curtain' speech.	Bertrand Russell, *History of Western Philosophy*. Sartre, *Existentialism and Humanism*. Eugene O'Neill, *The Iceman Cometh*. Jean Cocteau, *La Belle et la Bête*
1947	India becomes independent. Chuck Yeager breaks the sounds barrier.	Tennessee Williams, *A Streetcar named Desire*. Albert Camus, *The Plague*. Anne Frank, *The Diary of Anne Frank*.
1948	In South Africa, Apartheid legislation passed. Gandhi is assassinated. State of Israel founded.	Brecht, *The Caucasian Chalk Circle*. Greene, *The Heart of the Matter*.
1949	NATO formed. Republic of Ireland formed. Mao proclaims China a People's Republic.	George Orwell, *1984*. Simone de Beauvoir, *The Second Sex*. Arthur Miller, *Death of a Salesman*.
1950	Schuman Plan. Korean War begins. China conquers Tibet. First successful kidney transplant.	In US, McCarthyism starts (to 1954). Billy Wilder, *Sunset Boulevard*.
1951	Anzus pact in Pacific.	J D Salinger, *The Catcher in the Rye*
1952	Gamal Abdel Nasser leads coup in Egypt. US tests hydrogen bomb. Elisabeth II becomes queen of Britain. McCarthy era begins in US.	Michael Tippett, *The Midsummer Marriage*. Hemingway, *The Old Man and the Sea*. Samuel Beckett, *Waiting for Godot*. *High Noon* (starring Gary Cooper and Grace Kelly)
1953	Stalin dies. Mau Mau rebellion in Kenya. Eisenhower becomes US president. Korean War ends. Francis Crick and James Watson discover double helix (DNA).	Dylan Thomas, *Under Milk Wood*. Arthur Miller, *The Crucible*. Federico Fellini, *I Vitelloni*.

Year	Age	Life
1954	46	Merrill retires from films for the next six years.
1955	47	Davis returns to Hollywood to reprise her role as Queen Elizabeth I in *The Virgin Queen*, which does poorly at the box office.
1956	48	Davis stars in *Storm Center* and *The Catered Affair*, both box-office bombs.
1957	49	While rehearsing for stage adaptation of *Look Homeward, Angel*, Davis falls and hurts her back; leaves Merrill for the first time. Returns by Christmas, which the family spends in Maine for the last time.
1958	50	Davis leaves with daughter and sister for Europe, where she makes two more unsuccessful movies, *John Paul Jones* and *The Scapegoat*.
1959	51	Bobby Davis diagnosed with manic-depressive syndrome. Davis and Merrill split after explosive collaboration on *The World of Carl Sandburg*.
1960	52	Merrill-Davis divorce finalised. Lengthy custody hearings ensue.
1961	53	1 July: Ruthie Davis dies on what would have been her 53rd wedding anniversary. Davis appears in Frank Capra's *A Pocketful of Miracles* and Tennessee Williams's *The Night of the Iguana*.
1962	54	Davis places incendiary want ad; stars with her old rival, Joan Crawford, in *Whatever Happened to Baby Jane?* for which Davis receives her last Oscar nomination.
1963	55	16-year-old BD Sherry meets Jeremy Hyman at the Cannes film festival that summer; they exchange vows in December. To pay for a lavish wedding, Davis makes her first picture exclusively for money, *Where Love Has Gone*.
1964	56	Davis stars as twins once again in *Dead Ringer;* makes abominable movie in Italy, *The Empty Canvas*. Davis moves to Connecticut to be near her daughter and Hyman. Davis attempts to revive the success of *Baby Jane* in *Hush, Hush . . . Sweet Charlotte*.

Year	History	Culture
1954	Ho Chi Minh forms government in North Vietnam.	Kingsley Amis, *Lucky Jim*. J R R Tolkien, *The Lord of the Rings*.
1955	West Germany joins NATO. Warsaw Pact formed.	Tennessee Williams, *Cat on a Hot Tin Roof*. Vladimir Nabokov, *Lolita*
1956	Suez Crisis. Revolts in Poland and Hungary. Castro and 'Che' Guevara land in Cuba.	Lerner (lyrics) and Loewe (music), *My Fair Lady*. Elvis Presley, 'Heartbreak Hotel'. John Osborne, *Look Back in Anger*.
1957	Treaty of Rome: EEC formed. USSR launches Sputnik 1. Ghana becomes independent.	The Academy excludes anyone on the Hollywood blacklist from consideration for Oscars (to 1959).
1958	De Gaulle becomes president. Great Leap Forward in China. Castro leads revolution in Cuba.	Boris Pasternak, *Dr Zhivago*. Claude Lévi-Strauss, *Structural Anthropology*. Harold Pinter, *The Birthday Party*.
1959	In US, Alaska and Hawaii are admitted to the union. Bandaranaike (Sri Lanka) is assassinated.	Motown Records founded. Buddy Holly dies in plane crash. *Ben Hur* (dir. William Wyler). Günter Grass, *The Tin Drum*
1960	Vietnam War begins (until 1975). OPEC formed. Oral contraceptives marketed.	Fellini, *La Dolce Vita*. Alfred Hitchcock, *Psycho*
1961	Berlin Wall erected. Bay of Pigs invasion. Yuri Gagarin is first man in space.	The Rolling Stones are formed. Rudolf Nureyev defects from USSR.
1962	Cuban missile crisis. Jamaica, Trinidad and Tobago, and Uganda become independent.	Edward Albee, *Who's Afraid of Virginia Woolf?* David Lean, *Lawrence of Arabia*
1963	J F Kennedy assassinated; Martin Luther King leads March on Washington. Kenya becomes independent.	Betty Friedan. *The Feminine Mystique*. The Beatles, 'She Loves You'. *Cleopatra* (Richard Burton and Elizabeth Taylor).
1964	Khruschev ousted by Leonid Brezhnev. First race relations act in Britain. Civil Rights Act in US. PLO formed. Word processor invented.	Harnick (lyrics) and Bock (music) *Fiddler on the Roof*. Saul Bellow, *Herzog*. Stanley Kubrick, *Doctor Strangelove*

Year	Age	Life
1965	57	Davis stars in another horror film, *The Nanny*.
1968	60	Davis hires her first live-in assistant, Vik Greenfield, who stays with her off and on for 8 years. Stars as another forgettable ghoul in *The Anniversary*.
1969	61	Davis is excluded from the birth of her first grandson, Ashley Hyman. Stars in her first all-location feature, *Bunny O'Hare*, a project Davis despises.
1971	63	Margot Merrill turns 20 at the Lochland School; Davis loses contact with her adopted daughter.
1972	64	Davis returns to the stage for the first time in 11 years, in Joshua Logan's *Miss Moffat*. Over the next few years, in an attempt to stabilise her finances, Davis makes three more television pilots, none of which is picked up as a series: *Madame Sin, The Judge and Jake Wyler*, and *Hello Mother Goodbye!*
1973	65	After graduating from college, Michael Merrill weds high school sweetheart, Chou Chou Snow; BD fails to attend ceremony. Davis tours America, England, and Australia in *The Bette Davis Show*, a retrospective of her career. Davis lists her annual income as $26,000 and applies for social security benefits.
1976	68	Davis wins Emmy for her role in the television drama, *The Disappearance of Aimee*, in which she starred opposite Faye Dunaway.
1977	69	Davis becomes first woman ever to receive a Lifetime Achievement Award from the Film Institute; BD declines to attend. August: BD gives birth to Justin Hyman.
1978	70	Makes *Death on the Nile* in Egypt. December: after another dispute with BD, Davis leaves Connecticut and moves back to Hollywood.
1979	71	Davis hires 22-year-old Kathryn Sermak as her personal assistant; Sermak soon becomes the most important person in the actress's life.

Year	History	Culture
1965	Military coup in Indonesia.	Neil Simon, *The Odd Couple*.
1968	Tet Offensive. In US, M L King and Robert Kennedy assassinated. In Paris, student riots.	Kubrick, *2001: A Space Odyssey*. The Rolling Stones, *Beggar's Banquet*.
1969	Neil Armstrong takes first moon walk. Internet created by US Department of Defence. Massive anti-war rallies in US.	Mario Puzo, *The Godfather. Easy Rider* (Dennis Hopper and Peter Fonda). *Midnight Cowboy* becomes first wide-released X-rated film.
1971	In Uganda, Idi Amin seizes power. Nixon proclaims end of US offensive role in Vietnam War.	Dmitri Shostakovich, *Symphony No. 15*. Solzhenitsyn, *August 1914*. Kubrick, *A Clockwork Orange*
1972	In US, Watergate scandal. Bloody Sunday massacre (N Ireland). Allende overthrown in Chile; Pinochet takes power. World Trade Centre completed.	Richard Adams, *Watership Down*. Bertolucci, *Last Tango in Paris*. Francis Ford Coppola, *The Godfather*
1973	Yom Kippur War. Denmark, Ireland and Britain enter EC. US withdraws from Vietnam War. OPEC oil crisis.	Pink Floyd, *The Dark Side of the Moon*. Larkin, *High Windows*. E F Schumacher, *Small is Beautiful*. Truffaut, *Day for Night*
1976	Chairman Mao dies. Soweto massacre.	Alex Haley, *Roots*
1977	Jimmy Carter inaugurated US president. Democratic elections in Spain . Deng Xiaoping assumes power in China.	The Sex Pistols, 'God Save the Queen'. George Lucas, *Star Wars*. Elvis Presley dies.
1978	Pope John Paul II elected. Camp David Accord. First test-tube baby born.	John Irving, *The World According to Garp*. Michael Cimino, *The Deer Hunter*. First broadcast of *Dallas*.
1979	In UK, Thatcher becomes PM. Civil war in El Salvador. Iranian revolution. Soviet Union invades Afghanistan. Pol Pot deposed in Cambodia.	Milan Kundera, *The Book of Laughter and Forgetting*. V S Naipaul, *A Bend in the River*. Woody Allen, *Manhattan*

Year	Age	Life
1980	72	Davis celebrates her 50th anniversary of her first appearance on film in the Disney movie, *The Watcher in the Woods*. Stars with her grandson Ashley in the made-for-TV movie, *Family Reunion*. Bobby Davis dies from breast cancer.
1983	75	Diagnosed with breast cancer, Davis undergoes a radical mastectomy.
1984	76	Davis returns to work, co-starring with Helen Hayes in the TV movie of Agatha Christie's *Murder with Mirrors*.
1985	77	BD Hyman converts to evangelical Christianity; publishes the scandalous memoir, *My Mother's Keeper*.
1987	79	Davis honoured at the Kennedy Center in Washington DC.
1989	81	6 October: Davis dies in Paris on her way back from a film festival in San Sebastian, Spain; estate divided between Kathryn Sermak and Michael Merrill.

Year	History	Culture
1980	Rhodesia independent (Zimbabwe). President Tito of Yugoslavia dies. Polish strikers occupy Lenin shipyard in Gdansk. In US, Reagan elected president.	Michael Jackson, *Thriller*. Richard Attenborough, *Gandhi*. Werner Herzog, *Fitzcarraldo*. Spielberg, *ET*
1983	Reagan proposes 'Star Wars' defence system for US. Polish worker Lech Walesa wins Nobel Peace Prize.	García Márquez, *Chronicle of a Death Foretold*. Alice Walker, *The Color Purple*
1984	Indira Gandhi assassinated by her Sikh bodyguard in revenge for troops storming temple.	Bruce Springsteen, *Born in the USA*. Milan Kundera, *The Unbearable Lightness of Being*
1985	Gorbachev calls for *glasnost* ('openness') in Soviet life and a policy of *perestroika* ('reconstruction')	Norman Foster: HSBC building, Hong Kong. Richard Rogers: Lloyds of London
1987	In US, Iran-Contra scandal	Margaret Atwood, *The Handmaid's Tale*.
1989	Students march on Beijing's Tiananmen Square to call for democracy. Mass demonstrations in Leipzig call for reforms: Berlin Wall is demolished.	Poet Vaclav Havel elected President of Czechoslovakia. Ayatollah Khomeini issues *fatwa* against Salman Rushdie.

Select Filmography

Between *Bad Sister* in 1931 and *Wicked Stepmother* in 1989, Bette Davis appeared in 87 films, as well as many television series and made-for-TV movies. Though she began her career as a stage actress, she had professional acting engagements in only 10 theatrical productions, 5 of which predated her arrival in Hollywood. The following feature and television films represent the highlights of Davis's career, available in good video shops and online. Starred items indicate films of particular interest.

Cabin in the Cotton, 1932
(Directed by Michael Curtiz; co-starring Richard Barthelmess)

Three on a Match, 1932
(Directed by Mervyn LeRoy; co-starring Joan Blondell and Ann Dvorak)

*Of Human Bondage, 1934
(Directed by John Cromwell; co-starring Leslie Howard)

Dangerous, 1935
Winner of Best Actress Academy Award (Directed by Alfred Green; co-starring Franchot Tone and Margaret Lindsay)

*The Petrified Forest, 1936
(Directed by Archie Mayo; co-starring Leslie Howard and Humphrey Bogart)

*Marked Woman, 1937
(Directed by Lloyd Bacon; co-starring Humphrey Bogart and Jane Bryan)

Kid Galahad, 1937
(Directed by Michael Curtiz; co-starring Edward G Robinson and Humphrey Bogart)

Jezebel, 1938
Winner of Best Actress Academy Award (Directed by William Wyler; co-starring Henry Fonda and George Brent)

Dark Victory, 1939
Nominated for Best Actress Academy Award (Directed by Edmund Goulding; co-starring George Brent, Geraldine Fitzgerald, Humphrey Bogart and Ronald Reagan)

Juarez, 1939
(Directed by William Dieterle; co-starring Paul Muni, Brian Aherne and Claude Rains)

The Old Maid, 1939
(Directed by Edmund Goulding; co-starring Miriam Hopkins and George Brent)

The Private Lives of Elizabeth and Essex, 1939
(Directed by Michael Curtiz; co-starring Errol Flynn and Olivia de Havilland)

All This, and Heaven Too, 1940
(Directed by Anatole Livtak; co-starring Charles Boyer)

The Letter, 1940
Nominated for Best Actress Academy Award (Directed by William Wyler; co-starring Herbert Marshall and James Stephenson)

The Great Lie, 1941
(Directed by Edmund Goulding; co-starring George Brent and Mary Astor)

The Little Foxes, 1941
Nominated for Best Actress Academy Award (Directed by William Wyler; co-starring Herbert Marshall and Teresa Wright)

In This Our Life, 1942
(Directed by John Huston; co-starring Olivia de Havilland and George Brent)

Now, Voyager, 1942
Nominated for Best Actress Academy Award (Directed by Irving Rapper; co-starring Paul Henreid and Claude Rains)

Old Acquaintance, 1943
(Directed by Vincent Sherman; co-starring Miriam Hopkins)

Mr Skeffington, 1944
Nominated for Best Actress Academy Award (Directed by Vincent Sherman; co-starring Claude Rains)

The Corn Is Green, 1945
(Directed by Irving Rapper; co-starring John Dall)

A Stolen Life, 1946
(Directed by Curtis Bernhardt; co-starring Glenn Ford and Walter Brennan)

Deception, 1946
(Directed by Irving Rapper; co-starring Paul Henreid and Claude Rains)

Winter Meeting, 1948
(Directed by Bretaigne Windust; co-starring James Davis)

Beyond the Forest, 1949
(Directed by King Vidor; co-starring Joseph Cotton and David Brian)

All About Eve, 1950
Nominated for Best Actress Academy Award (Directed by Joseph L Mankiewicz; co-starring Anne Baxter and Gary Merrill)

Payment on Demand, 1951
(Directed by Curtis Bernhardt; co-starring Barry Sullivan)

The Star, 1952
(Directed by Stuart Heisler; co-starring Sterling Hayden and Natalie Wood)

The Virgin Queen, 1955
(Directed by Henry Koster; co-starring Richard Todd and Joan Collins)

A Pocketful of Miracles, 1961
(Directed by Frank Capra; co-starring Glenn Ford and Peter Falk)

*Whatever Happened to Baby Jane?, 1962
Nominated for Best Actress Academy Award (Directed by Robert Aldrich; co-starring Joan Crawford)

Hush, Hush . . . Sweet Charlotte, 1964
(Directed by Robert Aldrich; co-starring Olivia de Havilland)

Bunny O'Hare, 1971
(Directed by Gerd Oswald; co-starring Ernest Borgnine)

Death on the Nile, 1978
(Directed by John Guillermin; co-starring Maggie Smith and Angela Lansbury)

The Watcher in the Woods, 1980
(Directed by John Hough; co-starring Carroll Baker)

The Whales of August, 1987
(Directed by Lindsay Anderson; co-starring Lillian Gish)

TELEVISION

Madame Sin, 1972
(Directed by David Greene; co-starring Robert Wagner)

The Disappearance of Aimee, 1976
(Directed by Anthony Harvey; co-starring Faye Dunaway)

Hotel, 1983
(Directed by Jerry London)

Murder with Mirrors, 1985
(Directed by Dick Lowry; co-starring Helen Hayes)

Further Reading

AUTOBIOGRAPHIES, COLLECTIONS OF
INTERVIEWS AND FAMILY MEMOIRS

Bette Davis wrote two autobiographies, *The Lonely Life* with Sanford Dody (New York: 1961) and *This 'n' That* with Michael Hershkowitz (New York: 1987). The first covers, in greeting-card syntax, the actress's life up to her 1960 divorce from Gary Merrill. The second, dictated two years before Davis's death, is almost unreadable, with chapters divided by topic, including one on the Joan Crawford feud and another on men in Davis's life.

More entertaining are books of compiled interviews with the actress, who was a far more accomplished speaker than writer: Boze Hadleigh, *Bette Davis Speaks* (New York: 1996) and Whitney Stine, *I'd Love to Kiss You* (New York: 1990). Stine also wrote a tedious book chronicling only Davis's professional life, *Mother Goddam: the Story of the Career of Bette Davis* (New York: 1974), which includes Davis's italicised commentary after every paragraph.

BD Hyman, *My Mother's Keeper* (New York: 1985) is the tell-all memoir of growing up with Bette Davis by the actress's only biological child. It is hideously written and impossible to put down.

BIOGRAPHIES

Finding a biography of Bette Davis is not the difficulty: it is finding one worth reading through to the end. Of those listed, Barbara Leaming's *Bette Davis* (London: 1992) is far and away the most thoughtful and well-written biography of the actress.

Considine, Shaun, *Bette and Joan: The Divine Feud* (London: 1989): an extremely entertaining gimmick contrasting the lives of the Golden

Age's best-publicised rivals, Bette Davis and Joan Crawford.

Higham, Charles, *Bette Davis* (New York: 1981): like Lawrence Quirk's *Fasten Your Seatbelts*, this is an unreliable and gossipy account.

LaPlace, Maria 'Stars and the Star System: the Case of Bette Davis' in *The Film Studies Reader*, ed Joanne Hollows (London: 2000): an essay exploring Davis's significance to early feminists.

Leaming, Barbara, *Bette Davis* (London: 1992) is the best available biography of the actress, focusing on Davis's childhood, her acting style, and the reasons for her undoing.

Moseley, Roy, *Bette Davis: An Intimate Memoir* (New York: 1989): a first-person testimony to the intense fan-devotion Davis inspired – and also to the actress's own desperate cultivation of this devotion in her later life.

Quirk, Lawrence, *Fasten Your Seatbelts: The Passionate Life of Bette Davis* (New York: 1991): concentrates on the anecdotal side of Davis's film career and rumours of her deviant sexual practices – an extended gossip column which ranks scandal above accuracy.

Ringgold, Gene, *The Films of Bette Davis* (New Jersey: 1966): a handsomely illustrated compilation of plot synopses, critical responses, and film stills of Davis's films from *Bad Sister* (1931) to *The Nanny* (1965).

Spada, James, *More Than a Woman* (New York: 1993): in spite of its tabloid prose and sizzling invented dialogue to push the narrative along, this book is meticulously researched and includes useful interviews with Davis's co-workers and friends.

Staggs, Sam, *All About All About Eve* (New York: 2000): an exhaustive and surprisingly compelling 'biography' of what is arguably Bette Davis's most popular film, *All About Eve*. In what he describes as the 'complete behind-the-scenes story of the bitchiest film ever made,'

Staggs covers every angle of *Eve*, from the on-set altercations to the later careers of its stars.

GENERAL BOOKS ON HOLLYWOOD

Agee, James, *Agee on Film* (New York: 1958): the film critic for the *Nation* from 1942 to 1948 and *Time* from 1941 to 1948, Agee, who was also a screenwriter and novelist, was the American intelligentsia's most eloquent moviegoer.

Baxter, John, *Hollywood in the Thirties* (London: 1968): a brief and limpid account of the 'Hothouse atmosphere' of Hollywood filmmaking during its Golden Age.

Birdwell, Michael, *Celluloid Soldiers: The Warner Bros Campaign against Nazism* (New York: 1999): the fascinating story of Harry Warner's attempt to defend American values on celluloid.

Hoopes, Roy, *When the Stars Went to War* (New York: 1994): a history of Hollywood's involvement in World War Two, with some unexpected twists.

Kael, Pauline, *5000 Nights at the Movies* (New York: 1982) and *For Keeps* (New York: 1994): the *New Yorker*'s film critic until her death in 2001, Kael is the Golden Age authority who, like James Agee, elevated criticism of American film into an art.

Sklar, Robert, *Movie-Made America* (New York: 1975): the best general history of the rise and fall of Hollywood culture, from the first invention of the Kinetoscope to the rise of the independent producer in the 1970s.

Thomson, David, *The New Biographical Dictionary of Film* (New York: 2002): an uproarious and insightful encyclopaedia-style reference essential for its capsule-biographies of Davis, her co-workers, and her enemies.

Picture Sources

The author and publishers wish to express their thanks to the following sources of illustrative material and/or permission to reproduce it. They will make proper acknowledgemments in future editions in the event that any omissions have occurred.

Corbis: pp. 3, 26; Getty Images: pp. 17, 30, 33, 55, 56, 106, 108, 113; Lebrecht Picture Collection / Interfoto: pp. i iii, 21, 40, 45, 50, 53, 58, 69, 71, 72, 80, 93, 100, 103, 115, 118, 126; Topham Picturepoint: pp. 7, 13, 18, 39, 64, 130, 138, 141, 144.

Index

Huston, John, 83, 84
Hyman, Ashley, 131, 136, 138, 145
Hyman, Barbara Davis (BD) (née
    Sherry, then Merrill), 98, 104, 106,
    113, 116; changes name to Merrill,
    107; temper, 111; appears in
    Whatever Happened to Baby Jane?,
    123; relationship with mother,
    128–35; courtship and marriage,
    128–9; illnesses, 137–8; conver-
    sion, 138–9; last call to mother,
    144; omitted from Davis's will,
    145; *My Mother's Keeper*, 112,
    139–42; *Narrow Is the Way*, 141
Hyman, Jeremy, 128–31, 134, 136
Hyman, Justin, 134, 145

I Was a Member of a Chain Gang, 28
Ibsen, Henrik, 57, 91; *The Wild Duck*,
    11, 19–20

Jacobson, Dr Max, 110
Jolson, Al, 18; *The Jazz Singer*, 20,
    27–8
Jowitt, Sir William, 47–8

Kael, Pauline, 60, 63, 73, 125, 126
Kinetoscope, 1, 20
Know Your Enemy: Japan, 67
Kodak, 2

La Gallienne, Eva, 12
Laguna Beach, 97
Legion of Decency, 78
Leigh, Vivien, 63, 125
Life of Émile Zola, The, 67
Light, James, 18
Livtak, Anatole, 60
Lochland School, 112, 116
Lombard, Carole, 45
London, 47–8
Los Angeles, 32, 62, 70, 113, 134,
    135
Louisiana, 125
Lowell, Massachusetts, 2
Lumière brothers, 1

Maine, 111, 114
Maltese Falcon, The, 44
Mankiewicz, Joseph, 100–2
Marshall, Herbert, 82
Matthews, James, 54
Maugham, W Somerset: *Of Human
    Bondage*, 33; *The Letter*, 63, 78–9
Mayer, Louis B, 42
'Merrie Melodies', 89
Merrill, Barbara Davis (BD), *see*
    Hyman, Barbara Davis (BD)
Merrill, Gary, 102, 104–5, 108,
    117–18, 128; devotion to Margot,
    111–12; married life, 112; mar-
    riage breaks down, 113–16; *Bette,
    Rita, and the Rest of My Life*, 107,
    140
Merrill, Margot, 106; brain damaged
    and confined to institution,
    111–12, 116; omitted from Davis's
    will, 145
Merrill, Michael, 106, 111–14, 130;
    marriage and career, 132; benefici-
    ary of Davis's will, 145
Mexico, 70, 97, 104
MGM, 28, 121
Mildred Pierce, 74, 121
Millay, Edna St Vincent, 18
Mr Smith Goes to Washington, 56
Mitchell, Margaret, 52
Monroe, Marilyn, 17, 90; Davis on,
    102
Motion Picture Patents Company
    (Edison Trust), 1–2, 89
Motion Picture Producers and
    Distributors of America, 78
Muni, Paul, 13, 44, 57, 59–60, 74

LIFE & TIMES FROM HAUS

Churchill
by Sebastian Haffner
'One of the most brilliant things of
any length ever written about
Churchill.' *TLS*
1-904341-07-1 (pb) £9.99
1-904341-06-3 (hb) £12.99

Dietrich
by Malene Skaerved
'It is probably the best book ever on
Marlene.' C. Downes
1-904341-13-6 (pb) £9.99
1-904341-12-8 (hb) £12.99

Beethoven
by Martin Geck
'. . . this little gem is a truly handy
reference.' *Musical Opinion*
1-904341-00-4 (pb) £9.99
1-904341-03-9 (hb) £12.99

Prokofiev
by Thomas Schipperges
'beautifully made, . . . well-produced
photographs, . . . with useful
historical nuggets.' *The Guardian*
1-904341-32-2 (pb) £9.99
1-904341-34-9 (hb) £12.99

Curie
by Sarah Dry
'. . . this book could hardly be bettered'
New Scientist
selected as **Outstanding Academic Title**
by *Choice*
1-904341-29-2 (pb) £9.99

Einstein
by Peter D Smith
'Concise, complete, well-produced and
lively throughout, . . . a bargain at the
price.' *New Scientist*
1-904341-15-2 (pb) £9.99
1-904341-14-4 (hb) £12.99

Casement
by Angus Mitchell
'hot topic' *The Irish Times*
1-904341-41-1 (pb) £9.99

Britten
by David Matthews
'I have read them all – but none with as
much enjoyment as this.' *Literary Review*
1-904341-21-7 (pb) £9.99
1-904341-39-X (hb) £12.99

De Gaulle
by Julian Jackson
'this concise and distinguished book'
Andrew Roberts *Sunday Telegraph*
1-904341-44-6 (pb) £9.99

Orwell
by Scott Lucas
'short but controversial assessment . . .
is sure to raise a few eyebrows' *Sunday
Tasmanian*
1-904341-33-0 (pb) £9.99

Bach
by Martin Geck
'The production values of the book are
exquisite, too.'
The Guardian
1-904341-16-0 (pb) £9.99
1-904341-35-7 (hb) £12.99

Kafka
by Klaus Wagenbach
'One of the most useful books about Kafka
ever published' *Frankfurter Allgemeine
Zeitung*
1-904341-02 -0 (PB) £9.99
1-904341-01-2 (hb) £12.99

Dostoevsky
by Richard Freeborn
'. . . wonderful . . . a learned guide'
The Sunday Times
1-904341-27-6 (pb) £9.99

Brahms
by Hans Neunzig
'readable, comprehensive and
attractively priced'
The Irish Times
1-904341-17-9 (pb) £9.99

Verdi
by Barbara Meier
'These handy volumes fill a gap in the
market . . . admirably.' *Classic fM*
1-904341-05-5 (pb) £9.99
1-904341-04-7 (hb) £12.99

Armstrong
by David Bradbury
'generously illustrated . . . a fine and well-
researched introduction' George Melly
Daily Mail
1-904341-46-2 (pb) £9.99
1-904341-47-0 (hb) £12.99